God has gifted Ray in amazing ways. His newest book is a mixture between a call to action and an instruction manual on how to reach lost people. Every Christian should read *How to Make Sure God Hears Your Prayers*. You will be challenged and rightfully so. The church needs a wake-up call, and I believe this book to be just that. Thank you, Ray, for stepping on my toes—again.

Carl Kerby | president and founder, Reasons for Hope, www.rforh.com

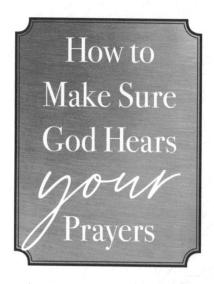

How to Make Sure God Hears *your* Prayers

Ray Comfort

BroadStreet
PUBLISHING

BroadStreet Publishing® Group, LLC
Savage, Minnesota, USA
BroadStreetPublishing.com

How to Make Sure God Hears Your Prayers
Copyright © 2023 Ray Comfort

9781424564712 (faux leather)
9781424564729 (ebook)

All video and email transcripts have been lightly edited for readability and clarity.

Stock or custom editions of BroadStreet Publishing titles may be purchased in bulk for educational, business, ministry, fundraising, or sales promotional use. For information, please email orders@ broadstreetpublishing.com.

Cover and interior by Garborg Design Works | garborgdesign.com

Printed in China

23 24 25 26 27 5 4 3 2 1

CONTENTS

FOREWORD

Despite Ray's nationality as a Kiwi from New Zealand and mine as an Aussie from Australia, we've been good friends for a long time (though we frequently tease and insult each other—a sign of affection in our culture!). When he asked me to write the foreword for his latest book, I was honored. Ray's resources are powerful and always point readers toward the most important message they could ever hear—the saving gospel of Jesus Christ.

Why should you read this book? Within its pages, Ray gives you the answer to your biggest problem. It's the biggest problem every single person who has ever lived has—the sin that separates us from a holy God. That sin is no small matter: "For the wages of sin is death" (Romans 6:23). We've rebelled against the Creator, and we deserve death (both physical death and eternal spiritual death) for our sin. But praise the Lord. He did what we can't do and provided a way of salvation. Consider the rest of Romans 6:23: "For the wages of sin is death, but the free gift of God is eternal life in Christ Jesus our Lord" (ESV).

Salvation is a free gift, provided by God's grace and offered to anyone who will turn from their sin and trust in Christ and his death and resurrection. Ray is passionate about this message because he truly loves people and wants to see everyone saved for eternity. That's why he has dedicated his life to daily sharing the message you'll read in this book.

So read *How to Make Sure God Hears Your Prayers* and honestly and seriously consider the truth that Ray shares. It's truth straight from the very Word of God, and it has the power to save you if you will repent and believe.

Ken Ham

CEO, Answers in Genesis, the Ark Encounter, and the Creation Museum

INTRODUCTION

When someone dies, we should ask ourselves if that person was a Christian. Did he know the Lord? Was she born again? These are legitimate ways to ask if the deceased person professed to believe in Jesus. However, the all-encompassing question we should ask is, *Did he or she* fear *the Lord?* It doesn't matter how much we accomplish in our lives, the size of our Christian ministry, or how much money we leave behind. Everything boils down to whether we fear God. This is because, while many people profess to be born again, only people who fear the Lord reflect that fear in how they live. The fear of God is the fertile soil from which good, biblical fruit grows, and as we shall see, it is a priceless gift from the hand of our loving Creator.

When a nation loses the fear of God, it doesn't depart from sin. And as with Israel of old, it instead gravitates toward idolatry. It creates its own image of God—one that won't and can't threaten future punishment for evil. That opens the gates to sexual sin, followed by general lawlessness—blasphemy, lying, stealing, greed, rape, violence, murder, pornography, pride, the delusion of self-righteousness, and even the killing of one's own offspring. Welcome to our modern-day world.

We desperately need to return to the preaching of truths that make sinners tremble. Such a thought may sound distasteful to some. However, in the light of Scripture, we should be suspicious of any medicine that isn't a little bitter. In addressing the necessity of the fear of the Lord, A. W. Tozer said,

> Wherever God appeared to men in Bible times the results were the same—an overwhelming sense of terror and dismay, a wrenching sensation of sinfulness and guilt. When God spoke, Abram stretched himself upon the ground to listen. When Moses saw the Lord in the burning bush, he hid his face in fear to look upon God. Isaiah's vision of God wrung from him the cry, "Woe is me!" and the confession, "I am undone; because I am a man of unclean lips."[1]

Abram, Moses, Isaiah, Daniel—even Jesus feared the Lord. Biblically speaking, the fear of God is an essential condition for a relationship with God. At first, it may be strange to consider that Jesus himself had a healthy fear of the Lord, but Scripture tells us that his prayers were heard by the Father not because of his faith or his humility of heart but "because of His godly fear" (Hebrews 5:7).

Every day millions pray, believing they are being heard by God. Some think they are heard because of their vain repetition or their many words. Others believe that nothing restricts the smallest prayer—that God always hears and responds. But Scripture says this is not so. It tells us that sin cuts us off from God so that he will not hear (see Psalm 66:18; Isaiah 59:1–2). If we want to capture God's attention, we must take note of the Bible's teaching on the subject and thoroughly mingle our prayers with the fear of God.

A book on the fear of the Lord goes against the tide of a culture that frowns on such talk. As far as the world is concerned, God is not to be feared. He is a loving Father who hears every prayer. But I must defend the integrity of Scripture with as much passion as I would defend the integrity of my faithful wife. While many of today's preachers don't delight in the fear of God, we must look to God's Word to see what he says about himself. That is my agenda with this publication.

Each of the chapters in this book concludes with a transcript of a real-life witnessing scene. As you will see, I use a biblical key to produce the fear of God in all those with whom I share the gospel. This is because I know they need the fear of the Lord to depart from sin, for it is "by the fear of the Lord men depart from evil" (Proverbs 16:6 KJV).

Having said all this, let me allay any possible concerns with a concession: there is a perversion of the doctrine of fear of the Lord, one that is neither biblical nor glorifying to God, and that has long been employed to keep the religious masses in submission. The fear of the Lord of which I am concerned is fear mingled with love—exemplified in the terrible cost of the cross. At that scene, we tremble.

May God bless you and strengthen you through this wonderful and sublime truth.

Ray Comfort
August 2021

Chapter 1

WHAT THE WORLD SAYS IS GOOD

There are over seven billion people on this earth right now. Many of them walk through their daily lives believing they are good people. Maybe they volunteer at the local nursing home or donate to orphanages. They may even attend church every Sunday. Yet when they pray, they wonder why God feels distant. They're "good" people after all. However, they don't fear the Lord. In secret, they sin because they don't think God notices or cares. But God cares deeply about our sin. It separates us from him.

SIN IN BELSHAZZAR'S COURT

While Daniel was faithfully serving God as an exile in Babylon, his captor, King Belshazzar, was partying. This was despite his city being surrounded by his enemy, the hostile Medo-Persian army, for four months. But he had a good reason not to be too concerned. Belshazzar had water and food enough to last for two decades. His city was encircled by two walls. The inner wall was twenty-one feet thick with massive towers at sixty-foot intervals. The outer wall was eleven feet in width and had watchtowers. Six feet outside these walls was a moat fed by the Euphrates River, making Babylon a seemingly impenetrable fortress.[2] Belshazzar, therefore, was unintimidated. He needed only wait until the enemy became discouraged and left, so despite the siege, he made a great feast for a thousand of his lords and calmly drank wine in their presence.

However, the God of Israel had already given the king a prophetic message:

> [Daniel] told the king three times that the kingdom of Babylon would end and that it would be replaced by the Medes and the Persians. The army outside the gates would win.
>
> God had also given the same message through other prophets. Both Isaiah and Jeremiah prophesied that Babylon would fall to the Medes (see Jeremiah 51:1–11; Isaiah 13:17–22). Isaiah's prediction was over 200 years earlier!
>
> Belshazzar knew what God had said, but he felt safe inside his city walls. In a final act of defiance, he threw a great party.[3]

His drinking of wine is mentioned five times in these few verses, inferring that this was more than just a feast. And one sin led to another. Scripture doesn't hesitate to align sexual sin with drunkenness. They are bedfellows: "Let us conduct ourselves properly and honorably as in the [light of] day, not in carousing and drunkenness, not in sexual promiscuity and irresponsibility" (Romans 13:13 AMP). The Bible further warns that drunkenness leads to sexual sin:

> For we have spent enough of our past lifetime in doing the will of the Gentiles—when we walked in lewdness, lusts, drunkenness, revelries, drinking parties, and abominable idolatries. (1 Peter 4:3)

Drunkenness emboldens sin by dulling the conscience. It muffles its warning and has no doubt robbed many men and women of virginity they otherwise would have prized. Drunkenness certainly marred Noah's good reputation (see Genesis 9:20–23).

Belshazzar's drunkenness not only led to sexual sin but also to idolatry, for it was while the king had a cup of wine in his hand that the now infamous and devilish thought entered his mind: he would take the cups from the temple so that he and his guests could drink wine from them:

While he tasted the wine, Belshazzar gave the command to bring the gold and silver vessels which his father Nebuchadnezzar had taken from the temple which had been in Jerusalem, that the king and his lords, his wives, and his concubines might drink from them. Then they brought the gold vessels that had been taken from the temple of the house of God which had been in Jerusalem; and the king and his lords, his wives, and his concubines drank from them. They drank wine, and praised the gods of gold and silver, bronze and iron, wood and stone. (Daniel 5:2–4)

But this wasn't solely for the pleasure of drinking fine wine. It was to be a time of praise to the demon gods of gold and silver, bronze and iron, wood and stone. And in Belshazzar's mind, they were worthy to be praised—because dumb idols don't forbid sexual sin. His idols let him behave however he pleased. The psalmist speaks of how the ungodly boast of their idols: "Let all be put to shame who serve carved images, who boast of idols" (Psalm 97:7).

Sinners feel so safe and secure from the judgment of God that they throw a party. Despite the many warnings in Scripture, the voice of conscience, and the protest of the church against sin, people today have fortified themselves behind impenetrable walls and become emboldened in their sin, just like Belshazzar: "Yet they say, 'The LORD does not see, nor does the God of Jacob understand'" (94:7).

All the while, justice strains against the reins of mercy. Despite the patience of God, his law remains. His love of justice never changes, but the Scriptures tell us that he is rich in mercy. Like a good judge, he waits patiently because he wants to show mercy to a criminal. The judge waits for signs of remorse. And it's the same with our Creator. He waits, but all the while, wrath is being stored up; the ultimate stallion rises on its hind legs and is keen to rush into battle:

> But in accordance with your hardness and your impenitent heart you are treasuring up for yourself wrath in the day of wrath and revelation of the righteous judgment of God, who "will render to each one according to his deeds": eternal life to those who by patient continuance in doing good seek for glory, honor, and immortality; but to those who are self-seeking and do not obey the truth, but obey unrighteousness—indignation and wrath, tribulation and anguish, on every soul of man who does evil. (Romans 2:5–9)

How can we not but tremble when we think of the terrifying fate of those who don't fear God—who, without restraint, give themselves to sin? They "feast…without fear," serving their own lusts. "They are clouds without water, carried about by the winds; late autumn trees without fruit, twice dead, pulled up by the roots; raging waves of the sea, foaming up their own shame; wandering stars for whom is reserved the blackness of darkness forever" (Jude 1:12–13). They act in rebellion against God's commands. These people could be your coworkers, your neighbors, your friends, and even your family members. Without the fear of the Lord, all await his judgment.

THE WORLD'S DEFINITION OF GOOD AND EVIL

But our world tries to say, "Surely you don't mean everyone who doesn't fear the Lord is destined for hell? What about the neighbor who bakes cookies for you? Or the cousin who's just had a hard life? Or the friend who goes out of her way to help people?"

If you ask the unsaved to define *evil*, you will find that most confine their definition to a mass murderer like Hitler—someone who was responsible for the slaughter of millions of people. Or they will point to Jeffrey Dahmer—a man who, between 1978 and 1991, molested seventeen men and boys, strangled them, dismembered them, and cannibalized them.[4] Most people wouldn't deny mass murderers are evil.

In fact, the dictionary says that to be *evil* means to be "profoundly immoral and wicked."[5] These two monsters adequately qualify for that definition. However, the dictionary's use of the word *profoundly* elevates evil above the reach of average sinners, completely ignoring God's moral standards. Even respected theologians miss the mark if they don't point to an objective standard when describing evil:

> Essentially, evil is a lack of goodness. Moral evil is not a physical thing; it is a lack or privation of a good thing. As Christian philosopher J. P. Moreland has noted, "Evil is a lack of goodness. It is goodness spoiled. You can have good without evil, but you cannot have evil without good." Or as Christian apologist Greg Koukl has said, "Human freedom was used in such a way as to diminish goodness in the world, and that diminution, that lack of goodness, that is what we call evil."[6]

Although these statements are true, they are obscure if *goodness* is also left without a clear definition. What may be goodness to one person may not be goodness to another. How profound is *profound*, and how good is *good*?

With these vague definitions of good and evil, it's no wonder most people today wonder why God feels distant to them. They may even think that as long as they're good people—living up to whatever their definition of good is—that God will hear their prayers and do whatever they ask. However, the Bible has clearly defined good from evil. This is why we must point to the law of God as the ultimate reference point for good and evil. Scripture says the law is perfect, holy, just, and good (Psalm 19:7; Romans 7:12). By it, we can measure evil. The law demanded that Hitler love the Lord his God with all of his heart, mind, soul, and strength and to love every Jew as much as he loved himself. If he saw an injured Jewish person, he was required to lovingly bathe his wounds, transport him to a place where he could find help, and pay for any and all costs incurred (see Luke 10:25–37). Scripture is clear that anyone who breaks God's commandments "shall be called least in the kingdom of heaven" (Matthew 5:19). To look the other way when someone is in such need is profoundly evil. The law thunders the truth about evil: "For out of the heart proceed evil thoughts, murders, adulteries, fornications, thefts, false witness, blasphemies" (15:19).

Despite this truth, the world's "philosophy and empty deceit" (Colossians 2:8) is born out of willful ignorance:

Understand, you senseless among the people;
and you fools, when will you be wise?
He who planted the ear, shall He not hear?
He who formed the eye, shall He not see?
(Psalm 94:8–9)

They willfully forget that God judged the world through the flood in the time of Noah. There are oceans of evidence that the earth was once flooded (including the fact that 70 percent of the earth is still covered in water), but sinful men and women refuse to study it because of the implications of divine judgment:

For this they *willfully* forget: that by the word of God the heavens were of old, and the earth standing out of water and in the water, by which the world that then existed perished, being flooded with water. But the heavens and the earth which are now preserved by the same word, are reserved for fire until the day of judgment and perdition of ungodly men. (2 Peter 3:5–7, emphasis added)

Without the law to bring knowledge of sin and the fear of the Lord, people cannot help but do that which is right in their own eyes. They are directed in a way that seems right by their own deficient moral compass, but that way only leads to death. No wonder people are so lost, and no wonder they are so lawless.

BEWARE OF BEING MISLED

Scripture says to beware! Be on your guard, for if you lack vigilance, you will be cheated! Stand your ground with both eyes peeled because "anyone" may try to fleece, hoodwink, mislead, and swindle you with worldly philosophy and empty deceit. That "anyone" could be your own loving mother or grandpa, gently correcting you by explaining that the God of the Bible is loving and kind and would never create hell, let alone damn anyone to such a place. They may even back up their thoughts by giving you a Bible verse about God being love. Or the "anyone" may be your science teacher, who leaves science for a moment or two to share her concern that "Christian fundamentalism," as she calls it, has led to tremendous bigotry and narrow-mindedness. The "anyone" may even be the convictions of a certain religion professor who says of evangelicals that "their racism, their sexism… their lack of belief in science, lack of belief and common sense may end up killing us all…If evangelicals don't change, they pose an existential crisis to us all."[7]

And "anyone" may even explain that the much-feared beliefs held by these evil and bigoted evangelicals can be traced back to the Bible. They blame the Bible because it speaks the truth about sin and sexual perversion, warning that God will judge the world in righteousness. That's why wicked people hate the Scriptures. So be on the alert for the friendly delivery person who gently tells you to let go of the vindictive God portrayed in that archaic book—a book, he'll tell you, that has been changed many times down through the ages. Be wary of the celebrity who unashamedly thanks God for her award but explains that she believes in an inclusive Jesus. Such love and tolerance for everyone is not only applauded by her fans but by all of Hollywood. However, the accolades would cease in a second if she were loving enough to warn them that God is intolerant of all sin:

> For this you know, that no fornicator, unclean person, nor covetous man, who is an idolater, has any inheritance in the kingdom of Christ and God. Let no one deceive you with empty words, for because of these things the wrath of God comes upon the sons of disobedience. Therefore do not be partakers with them. (Ephesians 5:5–7)

Simply quoting these two verses in an acceptance speech would stir Hollywood's demons of hatred and ensure blacklisting. It is indeed a sin in the world's eyes to share these truths.

Israel Folau learned this the hard way when, in 2019, Australian rugby union authorities suspended him from playing and later ended his contact for posting on his Instagram account several Bible verses about repentance.

The post's graphic listed various sins from 1 Corinthians 6:9, including drunkenness and idolatry, that people must repent of or face eternal judgment. Folau wrote that Jesus loves those who are living in sin and is giving sinful people time to repent, adding Galatians 5:19–21 and Acts 17:30.[8]

Sinners hate the light—no matter whom it shines through. But their philosophy is nothing new. It is the same venom that came through the vipers who hated Jesus two thousand years ago because he talked about them being evil (see John 7:7). Their worldview is "according to the basic principles of the world, and not according to Christ" (Colossians 2:8). Jesus was not shy in talking about the coming judgment:

> Most assuredly, I say to you, he who hears My word and believes in Him who sent Me has everlasting life, and shall not come into judgment, but has passed from death into life. Most assuredly, I say to you, the hour is coming, and now is, when the dead will hear the voice of the Son of God; and those who hear will live. For as the Father has life in Himself, so He has granted the Son to have life in Himself, and has given

Him authority to execute judgment also, because He is the Son of Man. Do not marvel at this; for the hour is coming in which all who are in the graves will hear His voice and come forth— those who have done good, to the resurrection of life, and those who have done evil, to the resurrection of condemnation. (John 5:24–29)

THE GRAVITY OF OUR SIN

While God's anger is like a flood pressing against a cracked dam, waiting to crush those beneath it—those who live without fearing his power—the Scriptures make a wonderful promise to those who do fear him: "As a father pities his children, so the LORD pities those who fear Him…But the mercy of the LORD is from everlasting to everlasting on those who fear Him, and His righteousness to children's children" (Psalm 103:13, 17).

Perhaps if we were to think differently about lost sinners, we would be struck with the seriousness of their plight. Consider this story D. L. Moody shared about the urgency to preach the gospel to our own children. While we must be concerned with our family, this story applies to all who don't fear God because every soul is precious to God:

There was a little story going the round of the American press that made a great impression upon me as a father. A father took his little child out into the field one Sabbath, and, it being a hot day, he lay down under a beautiful shady tree. The little child ran about gathering wild flowers and little blades of grass, and coming to its father and saying, "Pretty! pretty!" At last the father fell asleep, and while he was sleeping the little child wandered away. When he awoke, his first thought was, "Where is my child?" He looked all around, but he could not see him. He shouted at the top of his voice, but all he heard was the echo of his own voice. Running to a little hill, he looked around and shouted again. No response! Then going to a precipice at some distance, he looked down, and there upon the rocks and briars, he saw the mangled form of his loved child. He rushed to the spot, took up the lifeless corpse and hugged it to his bosom, and accused himself of being the murderer of his child. While he was sleeping his child had wandered over the precipice. I thought as I heard that, what a picture of the church of God![9]

Every lost person is like that child caught up in carefree play, not realizing that they are perhaps but a few steps away from a deadly precipice. Now is the time to chase after them and share the good news of salvation. Now is the time to plead with them for their eternal destiny. Now is the time to tell them they have good reason to be afraid!

WITNESSING ENCOUNTER

In the following conversation, see how knowledge of sin and its consequences gives an agnostic and an atheist something to think about.

RAY: What are your thoughts on the afterlife?

DAVID: I don't think much about it.

RAY: Are you agnostic?

DAVID: I guess if you had to classify me, that's probably what it would be.

KEN: I'm honestly a man of science, and I believe that we're just made out of molecules, and we come and go.

RAY: You've got a van there.

DAVID: Yeah.

RAY: Okay. Anyone make your van?

DAVID: Yes.

RAY: How do you know?

DAVID: How do I know that they made it?

RAY: Yes, I mean, what would you think of me if I said, "I don't know if anyone made this van?" You'd think I was a bit slow in the brain. Obviously, the thing's made. It's got design. It's got purpose. It's got wheels, steering wheel, motor. Everything in it says, "Hey, there was a maker of this van."

DAVID: Okay.

RAY: And when you look around you...

DAVID: There's also a clear history of developing the skills and the materials to make that van.

RAY: Yes, but even a kid who doesn't understand that would say, "Oh, the van's got a maker." He wouldn't say it came together from an explosion or something. So you don't need to know the history of van makers to know that someone made the van. Same with your T-shirt. Someone designed your T-shirt.

DAVID: Okay.

RAY: Everything designed has a designer. Everything made had a maker. So look at flowers, birds, trees, puppies, kittens, the seasons, the sun, the moon, the stars, the human eye with 137 million light-sensitive cells. Everything is designed impeccably, from the atom to the universe.

KEN: Okay.

RAY: So, now do you know God exists?

DAVID: Everyone I've ever met who would say that God exists, that there's a Creator, says that there's Adam and Eve and that Adam and Eve looked just like me.

RAY: No, Eve didn't.

DAVID: Well, Eve didn't. And that a snake came down and talked, and a bush really burned, and all this stuff. And I'm waiting for the person to come to me and say, "Hey, no, that really didn't happen. Those are all metaphors and stories to get you to think. But that's not really how it happened. That's just a story." If someone came to me with that, I'd listen.

RAY: Well, what you're saying makes sense. The Bible's full of crazy-sounding stories, really weird. You've only touched on a few of them.

DAVID: I know. [Laughs]

RAY: There's the opening of the Red Sea, there's Balaam's donkey—

DAVID: Yes, there is.

RAY: —that talked, there's Joshua stopping the sun, there's the walls of Jericho that came down, Jonah being swallowed by a big fish and coming back out three days later. All of it's really weird, and it's hard to swallow, including the Jonah story. So my agenda isn't to convince you the Bible's the Word of God. I'd be silly to try and do that because it is full of fantastic stories, in the truest sense of the word. My agenda is something else; it's to show you you're in terrible danger. Do you believe in God's existence?

KEN: Um, no.

RAY: So you believe the scientific impossibility that nothing created everything? Is that really what you believe? That's scientifically impossible! Nothing can't create anything because it's nothing. Can you see what I'm saying?

KEN: That makes sense, but I feel like it's just all, like, one big coincidence that everything just, like, started existing. I wouldn't believe in something I haven't seen before.

RAY: So you don't believe in love? Or wind? Or history? Or molecules?

KEN: That's a good point.

RAY: Yes, there's a lot of things we believe in that we can't see. Do you know what a colloquialism is?

KEN: Um, no.

RAY: Let me give you a couple of baseball colloquialisms like, *I want to throw you a curveball.*

Firstly, I want to touch base with you, throw you a curveball, and see if you can knock it out of the park.

KEN: Mm-hmm.

RAY: They're colloquialisms. They mean something. Even though they're about baseball, we know they mean something else. The *curveball* means a difficult question, *touch base* means I want to talk to you about something, and *hit it out of the park* means that I want you to do something that's going to impress me. Ever heard the colloquialism *He doesn't have a hope in hell*?

KEN: No.

RAY: You never heard that?

KEN: Never heard of it.

RAY: Yes, it's an American colloquialism, and it means that you don't have any hope at all, no hope in hell. So do you think you're a good person? If heaven exists, are you going to make it there?

KEN: If it exists, um…probably not.

RAY: So, you're doing things you know are morally wrong?

KEN: I guess, from the Ten Commandments, I've probably, like, broken a couple.

RAY: Like lying and stealing?

KEN: Yes.

RAY: So you're a lying thief?

KEN: I guess you could call me that.

RAY: Well, there would be a reason to want to run and hide from God. As Adam ran from God and hid, we want to do the same thing. Have you ever used God's name in vain? That's the third commandment.

KEN: Yes.

RAY: Would you use your mother's name as a cuss word?

KEN: No.

RAY: Of course not. Now tell me why you wouldn't do that.

KEN: Because she's someone I respect.

RAY: You love your mother, and you wouldn't use her name as a cuss word. What an insult to her!

DAVID: Okay.

RAY: And yet you've taken the name of God and used it in the place of a filth word, which is called blasphemy—so serious, David, it's punishable by death in the Old Testament. I appreciate your patience with me. One to go.

DAVID: Okay.

RAY: Jesus said if you look at a woman and lust for her, you commit adultery with her in your heart [Matthew 5:28]. Have you ever looked at a woman with lust?

DAVID: Of course.

RAY: Have you had sex before marriage?

DAVID: Of course.

RAY: Okay, here's a summation. I'm not judging you; this is for you to judge yourself. You've told me you're a lying, thieving, fornicating, blasphemous, adulterer at heart. And you have to face God on judgment day. And here's the big *if*…

DAVID: I didn't say I had to face God on judgment day.

RAY: Here's the big *if*…If God judges you by the Ten Commandments—we've looked at four of them—on judgment day, would you be innocent or guilty?

DAVID: I would be guilty.

RAY: Heaven or hell?

DAVID: If that is the…or if those are the options?

RAY: When did you last look at pornography?

KEN: Uhh…this week.

RAY: That'll keep you from coming to God because you know you're doing wrong, and you know God frowns upon it.

DAVID: What I'm told is, I can simply say, "I accept Jesus as my Lord and Savior," and all of a sudden I'm in, and we're all good, whether or not I stole a candy bar or took a life. I have a little problem with that.

RAY: Well, I don't blame you because that's a fallacy.

DAVID: Yes.

RAY: It's not true.

DAVID: Okay.

RAY: That's called the American Gospel, and it's very pervasive, and it's filled the church with false converts. We've got a lot of people who say they're Christians, but their lives don't match it. So let me tell you what the Bible says and get your thoughts on it.

DAVID: Okay.

RAY: The Scriptures say all liars will have their part in the lake of fire [Revelation 21:8]. No thief, no blasphemer, no adulterer will inherit the kingdom of God [1 Corinthians 6:9–10]. It obviously doesn't concern you that if death seized upon you today, you'd end up damned by

God. But David, it concerns me. It horrifies me. I love you. I care about you. And the thought of you going to hell takes my breath away. Do you know what the Bible says death actually is? You've obviously got some sort of Christian background—do you remember that Bible verse that tells us what death is?

DAVID: No.

RAY: The wages of sin is death—Romans 6:23. Do you remember that?

DAVID: Mm-hmm.

RAY: It's a very famous verse. Death is wages that God pays you for your sins. It's like a heinous criminal. He's raped three girls, murdered them, and the judge says, "You've *earned* the death sentence. This is what's due to you; this is your wage." And God says, in his eyes, sin is so serious, it demands the death sentence, capital punishment. The soul that sins, it shall die. And really, it horrifies me, the thought that you'd end up in hell. The second part of that verse is—it kind of brings some light to that darkness—it says the wages of sin is death, but the gift of God is eternal life through Jesus Christ our Lord. And it doesn't come through inviting Jesus into your heart. It comes by another means.

KEN: I don't think anyone's ever been either in heaven or hell, so I don't think anyone could decide which one is good or bad. And—

RAY: Are you sure of that?

KEN: Yes.

RAY: Well, I'll tell you where you're wrong. Every person who's been born again, who's become a Christian, has experienced the supernatural. The God who made all things reveals himself to you by transforming your life on the inside, so you love righteousness and hate that which is wrong.

KEN: Mm-hmm.

RAY: So every person who's become a Christian—a genuine biblical Christian—knows God exists because they know him, and they know his Word is true. Have you ever read the Bible?

KEN: Before.

RAY: Yes, it's full of prophecies that show the fingerprint of God all over his Word, and the Bible warns again and again that hell exists. It says there's going to be a time of retribution, a day of punishment. God's appointed a day in which he'll judge the world in righteousness. And you used to read the Bible?

KEN: Mm-hmm.

RAY: And you gave your heart to Jesus when you were a little kid?

KEN: Taught to.

RAY: Yes, and then you fell away when the hormones kicked in and girls looked a little more exciting than Noah's ark.

KEN: Um…as I got older, I had a more—different perspective of…

RAY: Yes, yes, the sin looks attractive. You're like the prodigal son. Now tell me, what did God do for guilty sinners so we wouldn't have to end up in hell. Do you remember?

KEN: Yes. Jesus died for us, so…

RAY: Most people know that, but they don't know this—and if you can get a grip of this, it'll change everything.

DAVID: Hmm, yes.

RAY: You and I broke God's law, the Ten Commandments; Jesus paid the fine. That's what happened on the cross. That's why his last words were, "It is finished" [John 19:30]. In other words, the debt has been paid. You've got to admit they're weird words to say when you're dying. Last words? "It is finished"? But he was saying the fine has been paid. It's like in a court of law, a judge can dismiss your case, let you go, if someone pays your fine. So, he can say, "Ken, there's a stack of speeding fines. This is deadly serious, but someone's paid them. You're free to go." And he can do that which is legal and right and just. You walk—even though you're guilty— because someone paid your fine.

And even though you and I are guilty of heinous crimes against God—very serious crimes worthy of the death sentence—God says, "You can walk. I'll let you live forever, legally, because of what Jesus did on the cross, paying the fine in his life's blood." Then he rose from the dead and defeated death. Simply repent of your sins, let them go, say, "God, forgive me," and don't play the hypocrite. Be a genuine Christian. Don't lie and steal and fornicate and say you're a Christian; that's just deceiving your-self. So, your repentance must be sincere and genuine—and then trust in Jesus like you trust a parachute.

Dave, you're on the edge of a plane ten thousand feet up, and you say, "I don't care if I die. You know, I can flap my arms and defeat this invisible gravity thing." I'd say, "Man, the best thing I can do for you would be to hang you out the plane by your ankles for five seconds," and you'd come in and say, "Man, give me a parachute," because fear has done its work.

DAVID: Okay, that makes sense.

RAY: And I've tried to hang you out in eternity just for a few minutes and say, "Dave, this is your soul, this is your life, the most precious possession you've got. Please think about it, let fear work for you; let it be your friend so you think about your eternity."

DAVID: Good points.

RAY: And you said about your children—obviously you love them so much—well, you don't want to lead them into death and hell, with no hope. You know, to die a hopeless death is like jumping out of a plane with no parachute. I'm seventy-one, coming up to seventy-two this year. The odds are I won't even make the end of this year. And you look at statistics...

DAVID: Naw, you look good. You're good. [Laughs] You've got a long time left.

RAY: You're very kind. I might make it to seventy-three.

DAVID: You're out in the sun, on a bike—those are good things.

RAY: Yes, but I want to say this to you, that when I do go, when the grim reaper comes for me, I've got no fear. The sickle's taken out of his hand. I came to this life with nothing, and I'm going to leave with my hand on the hand of Jesus. And nothing is as precious as that to me, and I just want to share that with you today. So will you think about what we talked about?

DAVID: I think it's very thoughtful and interesting, and I'm absolutely open to hearing all… things.

RAY: Well, I hope you'll go away from this and just think seriously about it, like if you were going to die tonight at midnight. Think of it that seriously.

DAVID: Okay.

RAY: With sobriety. Can I give you a book I wrote? I write books. It's called *Counting the Days*.[10] It's on Bible prophecy, signs of the end of the age. Can I give you a copy?

DAVID: Absolutely.

RAY: Would you read it?

DAVID: Sure.

RAY: Well, you've been very gracious. I know you haven't agreed with me on some points, but you've listened, and I really appreciate that. Are you going to think about what we've talked about?

KEN: Once in a while.

RAY: Okay, now let me see if I can speed up your "once in a while." Imagine if you knew for certain you were going to die tonight at midnight. And if you really believe that, everything within you would say, "Oh, I don't want to die!" That's your God-given will to live. It's so powerful, and you don't know it's there until your life is threatened. So I want you to think about it with that sense of sobriety, and think about my motive. Why am I talking like this? Because I love you. I know that your parents love you. They're praying for you. You're a prodigal son. You're out there enjoying the pig food [see Luke 15:16], and they want you to come home. God wants you to come home. He's going to change your heart the minute you say, "God, be merciful to me a sinner!" [Luke 18:13] and cause you to love that which is right instead of loving that which is pig food. Like the prodigal son. Is that making sense?

KEN: Yes.

RAY: You going to think about what we talked about?

KEN: Yes.

Chapter 2

A HEALTHY FEAR
OF THE LORD

One of our family's great blessings in life is to have
a chicken coop. It means we can give fresh eggs to
friends, neighbors, and family. One curse, however, is
that chickens attract rats. Over the years we have tried
almost everything to rid ourselves of these disease-
infested rodents to no avail. We did come close to
eradicating them once when a local company laid
traps and poisoned the rats. However, the California
authorities outlawed the effective rat poison, saying that it endangered the state's mountain lions.
Meanwhile, we continued to battle a small plague of
rats without any effective weapons to fight them.

The fear of the Lord is the only effective poison
that puts sin to death. But authorities within contemporary Christianity (many church leaders and pastors)
have outlawed it. Instead of preaching the holiness of

God and his consequential wrath and then pleading with sinners to flee to the cross, their message is insipid and unbiblical, irrelevant and ineffective. Many are more like motivational speakers rather than preachers of righteousness. The salt has lost its flavor and is good for nothing (see Matthew 5:13). Unable to find the truth within many churches, professing believers now find themselves alone in their battle with a sin-infested world, a sin-loving flesh, a plague of demons, and a devious devil—who "walks about like a roaring lion, seeking whom he may devour" (1 Peter 5:8).

As A. W. Pink once said,

> Time was when it was the custom to speak of a believer as a "God-fearing man;" that such an appellation has become nearly extinct only serves to indicate whither we have drifted. Nevertheless, it still stands written, "Like as a father pitieth his children, so the LORD pitieth them that fear him" (Psalm 103:13 [KJV]).[11]

God still commands us to fear the Lord even though most people around us have forgotten what being God-fearing men and women looks like. Good thing the Bible clearly defines what it means to live with the fear of the Lord.

MORE THAN AWE

While it is common to define the fear of God as reverential awe, the Bible tells us that we should not only have reverence but also "trembling" (Psalm 2:11). The King James Version of Psalm 4:4 reads, "Stand in awe, and sin not: commune with your own heart upon your bed, and be still. Selah." Albert Barnes, a nineteenth-century Presbyterian minister and theologian, offered the following commentary on this verse:

> The original word here [translated "Stand in awe"]—רגז râgaz—means to be moved, disturbed, disquieted, thrown into commotion; and as this may be by anger, fear, or grief, so the word comes to be used with reference to any one of these things…The connection here would seem to require that it should be understood with reference to "fear"—since we cannot suppose that the writer would counsel them to be moved or agitated by wrath or anger, and since there was no ground for exhorting them to be moved by grief. The true idea is, doubtless, that which is conveyed in our translation—that they were to fear; to stand in awe; to reflect on the course which they were pursuing, and on the consequences of that course, and by so doing to cease from their plans, and to sin no

further. God had determined to protect him whom they were engaged in persecuting, and, in prosecuting their plans, they must come into conflict with His power, and be overcome. The counsel, therefore, is just such as may properly be given to all men who are engaged in executing plans of evil.[12]

In other words, if we continue in sin we will come into conflict with God's power and be overcome, yet most of this world lacks this necessary fear. King David was complacent about his adultery and murder until he was put in a state of fear and trembling by the faithful rebuke of Nathan (see 2 Samuel 12:1–25). The Bible speaks of coupling fear with reverence. God should be held in reverence *and* is greatly to be feared: "God is greatly to be feared in the assembly of the saints, and to be held in reverence by all those around Him" (Psalm 89:7). Mere awe doesn't inspire people to turn from their sinful ways and repent. True godly fear does.

GODLY FEAR

Still, many people today, including Christians, wonder why we need to fear the Lord. Isn't he loving? Isn't he our comforter? While these characteristics are true of God, Scripture warns us of the error of forgetting he is also to be feared. The psalmist cries out to the Lord:

"My flesh trembles for fear of You, and I am afraid of Your judgments" (Psalm 119:120). Centuries later, Jesus instructed his followers to do likewise: "Do not fear those who kill the body but cannot kill the soul. But rather fear Him who is able to destroy both soul and body in hell" (Matthew 10:28).

A. W. Pink explained what true godly fear looks like in one of his messages:

> When we speak of godly fear, of course, we do not mean a servile fear, such as prevails among the heathen in connection with their gods. No; we mean that spirit which Jehovah is pledged to bless; that spirit to which the prophet referred when he said, "To this man will I (the Lord) look, even to him who is poor and of a contrite spirit, and trembleth at my word" (Isaiah 66:2 [KJV]).[13]

Similarly, Charles Spurgeon once illustrated how Noah lived his life with godly fear:

> Faith was the living principle, but fear was the moving power; for the text puts it, "By faith Noah, being warned of God of things not seen as yet, moved with fear." Faith molded him, but fear moved him. How was this? "I thought," says one, "that perfect love casts out fear." Yes, fear of a certain sort; but there is another fear

which perfect love embraces and nourishes. Noah had no evil fear. He had not a servile fear: he was not afraid of God as a culprit is afraid of a judge, or a convict of the hangman. He knew whom he believed, and was persuaded that he had a favour towards him.[14]

An accurate picture of God produces a healthy fear. During my many years of open-air preaching, I was approached by the police more than a dozen times. They were always firm and polite when they asked me to move along, and I was *always* compliant. I could have stood my ground by speaking about my First Amendment rights, but I never did. That's because of my upbringing. I was raised in New Zealand—at a time when the police didn't carry guns. When an American officer approached me, I never failed to say to myself, *He's got a gun!* I had more than mere respect for the officer's authority; it was a very real fear. I knew that if he felt threatened, he could justly kill me. And that's all it took to have me saying a polite, "Yes, sir" or "No, sir."

I have similar convictions about God even though he is much more powerful than a police officer with a firearm. Such thoughts continually help me to keep my evil heart from violating his law. This isn't because I'm striving for sinless perfection. Rather, it's because I have a propensity to sin (see Romans 7:17–20). I need the restraint of fear and trembling to keep me from going anywhere near the pleasures of sin. This sin is what can keep God from hearing our prayers. Isaiah 59:2 says, "Your iniquities have separated you from your God; and your sins have hidden His face from you, so that He will not hear." This doesn't mean that God is unaware of the prayer or somehow becomes deaf. The previous verse states, "The LORD's hand is not shortened, that it cannot save; nor His ear heavy, that it cannot hear." Rather, our sin creates a barrier between us and God. The fear of the Lord is what keeps us from our desire to sin.

CHARACTERISTICS OF A GOD-FEARER

As we have seen, we human beings are easily ensnared by sin. Our heads are easily turned by whispers from the world, the flesh, and the devil. Godly fear and trembling give us the incentive and motivation to stop toying with sin. The heart is too wicked to give it a slack leash. We should tremble in our sinful ways not only because of who God is but also because of the power he has to justly punish sinners. Heinous criminals should not only fear judges because of their robed status but more so because judges have the power to throw them into jail and toss away the key. A God-fearer understands God as both the judge of the sinful and the savior of those who obey him. Through Christ, we are clean in God's eyes, but in our daily walk, we easily soil our feet in this world. However, having a godly character doesn't mean we don't have temptations, but the truth of our character is revealed in what we *do* with those temptations.

When God gave the Ten Commandments to Israel, the Scriptures say, "And so terrifying was the sight that Moses said, 'I am exceedingly afraid and trembling'" (Hebrews 12:21). And it is with this combination of fear and trembling that we are to work out our own salvation (Philippians 2:12–13).

We are also to serve the Lord with this same fear and trembling (Psalm 2:11–12).

Psalm 15 exemplifies the life of a God-fearing person:

> O LORD, who may lodge [as a guest] in Your tent?
> Who may dwell [continually] on Your holy hill?
> He who walks with integrity and strength of character, and works righteousness,
> and speaks and holds truth in his heart.
> He does not slander with his tongue,
> nor does evil to his neighbor,
> nor takes up a reproach against his friend;
> in his eyes an evil person is despised,

but he honors those who fear the LORD [and
obediently worship Him with awe-inspired
reverence and submissive wonder].
He keeps his word even to his own disadvantage
and does not change it [for his own benefit];
he does not put out his money at interest [to a
fellow Israelite],
and does not take a bribe against the innocent.
He who does these things will never be shaken.
(Psalm 15:1–5 AMP)

According to these verses, those who fear God:

1. Will love righteousness. They will choose
   righteousness over sin when temptation
   comes.
2. Will strive to keep their thought-life pure.
3. Will refrain from gossip.
4. Will be kind and loving. The Scriptures say,
   "Love covers a multitude of sins" (1 Peter
   4:8 AMP). Notice the word *multitude*. Life
   is filled with annoyances. Neighbors have
   annoying dogs. Other drivers do cut in front
   of us. Friends and family can sometimes be
   thoughtless and unwittingly say things that
   hurt. If we start counting these "sins," we will
   end up with a multitude of transgressions
   that can steal our joy and leave us bitter.
   Such a result reveals a lack of love.

5. Will hate evil.
6. Will honor others who fear the Lord.
7. Will always keep his word.
8. Will never be greedy.

What Psalm 15 shows us is that everything we do, say, and think should be seasoned with the fear of the Lord: "Therefore, whether you eat or drink, or whatever you do, do all to the glory of God" (1 Corinthians 10:31). Commenting on Psalm 128:1, which says, "Blessed is every one who fears the LORD, who walks in His ways," Bunyan wrote that fearing the Lord is his highest duty:

> So that, considering that by the text we have presented to our souls the Lord God and Maker of us all, who also will be either our Saviour or Judge, we are in reason and duty bound to give the more earnest heed to the things that shall be spoken, and be the more careful to receive them, and put them in practice; for, as I said, as they present us with the mighty God, so they exhort us to the highest duty towards him; to wit, to fear him. I call it the highest duty, because it is, as I may call it, not only a duty in itself, but, as it were, the salt that seasoneth every duty. For there is no duty performed by us

that can by any means be accepted of God, if it be not seasoned with godly fear.[15]

The fear of the Lord is not a one-time event; it is a way of life. That's why it won't do to confuse the fear that is a torment with the fear that is the beginning of wisdom. One kills while the other makes alive. Then it keeps the forgiven sinner far from sin and close to Jesus. Therefore, fear and trembling are the key characteristics of the Christian life. We should love and cherish the title of God-fearer.

CHARACTERISTICS OF A GOD-SCOFFER

When Daniel was brought before the king, he reminded Belshazzar that all people "trembled and feared" before his grandfather—because of his frightening power (see Daniel 5:18–19). Daniel then said that although Belshazzar knew this, he did not humble his heart (v. 22). If a mere king was held in fear and trembling by all people because of his frightening power, how much more should we fear and tremble before God because of his infinitely greater and more frightening power? He was the one who gave Belshazzar's grandfather, Nebuchadnezzar, the power he had.

In the following chapter of Daniel, King Darius understood this "frightening power" when God famously delivered Daniel from the mouths of hungry lions. Look at the decree he then made:

> I make a decree that in every dominion of my kingdom men *must* tremble and fear before the God of Daniel.
>> For He is the living God,
>> and steadfast forever;
>> His kingdom is the one which shall not be destroyed,
>> and His dominion shall endure to the end.
>> (Daniel 6:26, emphasis added)

With this royal decree, all of Darius's subjects were charged to tremble and fear before the God of Daniel. But Belshazzar had no such response to God's power. Instead, he mocked and provoked God to anger. And so the hand of God broke through the heavens, and his holy finger wrote a short note that finally put terror into the heart of the king:

> In the same hour the fingers of a man's hand appeared and wrote opposite the lampstand on the plaster of the wall of the king's palace; and the king saw the part of the hand that wrote. Then the king's countenance changed, and his thoughts troubled him, so that the joints of his hips were loosened and his knees knocked against each other. (Daniel 5:5–6)

Notice that the hand appeared opposite the lampstand. The *Amplified Bible* spells out the importance of the hand writing on the wall opposite the lampstand:

> Suddenly the fingers of a man's hand appeared and began writing opposite the lampstand on [a well-lit area of] the plaster of the wall of the king's palace, and the king saw the part of the hand that did the writing. (v. 5)

God's promised judgment is in a well-lit area. He does not hide the consequences of our moral failures. He has given light to everyone (John 1:9). He once used his finger to write his commandments in stone (Exodus 31:18), and he also took the time to write the work of his law upon our hearts (see Romans 2:14–15). But when the king didn't respond to the light shining in his conscience and fear the Lord, God's finger gave him more light, and this mysterious divine message terrorized him:

> The king cried aloud to bring in the astrologers, the Chaldeans, and the soothsayers. The king spoke, saying to the wise men of Babylon, "Whoever reads this writing, and tells me its interpretation, shall be clothed with purple and have a chain of gold around his neck; and he shall be the third ruler in the kingdom." Now

all the king's wise men came, but they could not read the writing, or make known to the king its interpretation. Then King Belshazzar was greatly troubled, his countenance was changed, and his lords were astonished. (Daniel 5:7–9)

It's worthy to note that King Belshazzar specifically cried out for the astrologers, Chaldeans, and soothsayers:

At the height of the Babylonian Empire, the Chaldeans were an influential and highly educated group of people. Some historians believe that, after Persia conquered Babylon, the term Chaldean was used more often to refer to a social class of highly educated people than to a race of men. The Chaldeans influenced Nebuchadnezzar's decision to throw Shadrach, Meshach, and Abednego into the fiery furnace (Daniel 3:8) and were well known as wise men and astrologers during the time of Jewish captivity in Babylon. (Daniel 1:4; 2:10; 4:7; 5:7, 11).[16]

We tend to panic when nature does something strange. If the sky suddenly turned green, the sun turned blue, cats began barking like dogs, or the ocean drained to dry land, we would immediately turn to our experts for an explanation. Then, we'd breathe a sigh of relief when the mystery was solved. Take, for instance, a story about a time it was raining fish and frogs:

> In 1947, after a devastating storm, The Library of Congress reported that fish fell on a town in Louisiana. In more recent history, in 2005, people in Serbia reported thousands of frogs falling from the sky…Though this may seem like something out of the Bible, there is a scientific reason why this may occur.
>
> A tornado consists of a low-pressure area at the center of a high-pressure cone. When a tornado (or waterspout) forms over water, light-weight objects in the water, like frogs and fish, can be sucked up and carried over land. Once the waterspout hits land, it loses energy and slows down. This causes the pressure to drop and the vortex releases whatever it has been carrying. Including frogs.[17]

Rain of frogs and hogs or cats and dogs is frightening—until science reassures us that it isn't something supernatural. *We need not fear that this is some sort of judgment of God,* we tell ourselves, *because it can all be explained.* But humanity cannot escape death and judgment through worldly wisdom.

Belshazzar should have sought God's wisdom. God gave his law as a lamp to sinners: "For the commandment is a lamp, and the law a light" (Proverbs 6:23). The law of God gives us light. It's his divine finger that points out our sin and guilt (see Romans 3:19–20; 7:7, 13). It puts the writing on the wall for an evil world to see. When the law is used biblically, it produces a legitimate fear in our hearts. It halts the party, and makes our knees knock: "And as [Paul] reasoned of righteousness, temperance, and judgment to come, Felix trembled" (Acts 24:25 KJV).

The author of the book of Hebrews tells us, "Therefore, since we are receiving a kingdom which cannot be shaken, let us have grace, by which we may serve God acceptably with reverence and godly fear. *For our God is a consuming fire*" (Hebrews 12:28–29, emphasis added). That last phrase, "For our God is a consuming fire," tells us that God has the power to consume people like Belshazzar who continue to do evil:

> In flaming fire taking vengeance on them that know not God, and that obey not the gospel of our Lord Jesus Christ: Who shall be punished with everlasting destruction from the presence of the Lord, and from the glory of his power. (2 Thessalonians 1:8–9 KJV)

FEAR THAT LEADS TO MERCY

I am in awe as I watch a beautiful sunrise. The more I study the beams of light shining in every direction and stretching into the heavens with such amazing color, the more I'm in awe.

If such knowledge of the sun moves me from awe to terror, how much more should I tremble before the one who *made* that sun, along with all the other suns in the cosmos? Then add to that terror the sobering thought that sinners have filled him with wrath by their love of evil and that they will fall into his hands on the day of judgment. So why would we comfort sinners with worldly wisdom when they will one day face this judgment? The prodigal son had to leave the filth to return to his father. And that is the message we are to preach. We reason with others regarding sin, righteousness, the fear of the Lord, and the judgment to come—always heading for the good news of the cross and the mercy of God. We exist to tell the prodigal of the Father's steadfast love. They can turn to a God who hears them. Hear the joy expressed in this psalm by a God-fearer:

> If I had cherished sin in my heart,
> the Lord would not have listened;
> but God has surely listened
> and has heard my prayer.

Praise be to God,
who has not rejected my prayer
or withheld his love from me!
(Psalm 66:18–20 NIV)

When we see things as they really are, we will also come to see the gospel as the amazingly good news it really is! We will also live as the Bible has called us to, as joyful God-fearers who humbly obey God's commands in light of his stunning glory.

WITNESSING ENCOUNTER

This interview took place on Huntington Beach pier late in 2020. Dave didn't have an ounce of the fear of God, and that sparked a respectful verbal sparring.

RAY: Dave, do you think there's an afterlife?

DAVE: It all depends. I believe that everything is energy, and it'll all go back to energy.

RAY: So, you're going back to energy when you die?

DAVE: Of course. Everything is energy. Never can go away. It just changes forms.

RAY: Do you believe in God's existence?

DAVE: It all depends on how you define "God."

RAY: Well, the Creator of the universe; the One you have to stand in front of after you die. That One.

DAVE: Well, it all depends on how…that's not a very definite definition. How do you define God?

RAY: The Creator of the universe, the one that gave you a conscience.

DAVE: The universe is everything.

RAY: Yes, he created everything.

DAVE: I wouldn't say it's a "he."

RAY: What would you say it is?

DAVE: It's just a force.

RAY: Okay.

DAVE: The force of life.

RAY: Is this force happy with you or angry at you?

DAVE: It makes no difference; it doesn't really care.

RAY: Do you know what the first of the Ten Commandments is, Dave?

DAVE: Thou shall not kill.

RAY: No, that's the sixth.

DAVE: Okay, I guess I don't know—Oh, Thou shalt love your God and no other god shall come before him.

RAY: Yes, that's number one. You should not make yourself a false God. Don't make up a god to suit yourself. The first and second commandments say that. And when you say, "God's just the universe; he doesn't care about right and wrong," that's making up a god in your own image.

DAVE: So where are you getting your information?

RAY: The Bible.

DAVE: So, who says that I believe in the Bible?

RAY: Do you believe in the Bible?

DAVE: No.

RAY: Have you ever read it?

DAVE: Yes.

RAY: Give me a synopsis of the Bible in a couple of sentences, if you can.

DAVE: Love, love, love everybody, basically. It's basically about love and forgiveness. Loving God and loving forgiveness.

RAY: Well, in the Old Testament, God promised to destroy man's greatest enemy, death, and the New Testament tells us how he did it. Do you think you're a good person morally?

DAVE: Of course.

RAY: How many lies have you told in your life?

DAVE: I have no idea. Everybody's told lies. Even you have. If you don't admit that, then you're a liar again.

RAY: That's true. Have you ever stolen something?

Dave: I may have once or twice in my life. I'm not a thief.

RAY: Do you ever use God's name in vain?

DAVE: How do you define using God's name in vain?

RAY: Not giving it due honor or using it as a cuss word to express disgust, like "OMG" or just using God's name when you hurt yourself. Have you ever done that?

DAVE: I wouldn't call that using God's name in vain. I would call it using God's name in vain something like derogatory toward God himself, which is supposedly the only unforgivable sin. If you do believe in the Bible—the only unforgivable sin is to detest God and not accept God.

RAY: Jesus said that if you look at a woman and lust for her, you commit adultery with her in your heart [Matthew 5:28]. Have you ever looked at a woman with lust?

DAVE: I'm sure everybody has. I mean, I don't call it lust. I've looked at women before and thought they were desirable.

RAY: I'm not judging you. This is for you, not for me. But you've told me you're a lying thief, a blasphemer, and an adulterer at heart.

DAVE: No, I didn't. No, I didn't.

RAY: I thought you said everybody's committed those sins?

DAVE: Everybody's committed those sins once or twice. That doesn't make them bad. You could step on a bug, but that doesn't make you a killer.

RAY: But to the bug it does.

DAVE: It doesn't to anything else; you can't put such a broad blanket on something so petty and so small.

RAY: So here is the big question: If God judges you by the Ten Commandments on judgment day, are you going to be innocent or guilty?

DAVE: I don't care about your Ten Commandments.

RAY: I know that.

DAVE: I'm not a believer in all that.

RAY: That's why I'm talking to you, Dave. I care about you. I don't want you to end up in hell.

DAVE: So why do you keep dictating that to me when I don't care about that? It means nothing to me.

RAY: Because I want you to care. I want you to be safe from God's wrath. I don't want you to go to hell.

DAVE: That's what you want. That's not what I want.

RAY: That's why I'm talking to you. I want to change your mind.

DAVE: You're not going to change my mind. I'm a fifty-nine-year-old guy. I've been through all this stuff thousands of times.

RAY: Why did Jesus die on the cross? Do you know?

DAVE: Yes, of course, because he [expletive] Pontius Pilate.

RAY: No.

DAVE: He created trouble.

RAY: He came to suffer for the sin of the world.

DAVE: That's your opinion. The reality is that he [expletive] people off. Let me explain something to you. You say that God is all-forgiving, correct? Loving and all forgiving?

RAY: No, not at all.

DAVE: Oh, I thought you said that God is a loving God.

RAY: I didn't say that. You did.

DAVE: God is not a loving God? Is that what you're saying?

RAY: No, I'm saying that God isn't "all-forgiving."

DAVE: Are you saying that God is a loving God?

RAY: Of course.

DAVE: Then why in the world would he send people to hell? The people that he loves. You would never do that to anybody you loved, would you? Would you send them to hell for eternal damnation? Of course not.

RAY: Well, let me answer your question. God is also just and holy, and he'll by no means clear the guilty [Exodus 34:7].

DAVE: That's not just! There's nothing just about that.

RAY: Of course it is.

DAVE: No, that's not just. Just because somebody doesn't believe in you, that's not reason to send them to hell. I don't believe in what you're preaching right now, but is that any reason for me to send you to hell? Or to assault you? Or to do anything else like that to you? Or to torture you for eternity? No, that's not justice. That's not justification. No, that's not justification. That's [expletive].

RAY: God won't send you to hell for not believing something. He'll send you to hell for lying and stealing and adultery of heart and blasphemy.

DAVE: I don't lie and steal and commit adultery. I may have done it once or twice in my life, but I don't. That's not a common characteristic of me. People learn from their mistakes and move on.

RAY: Dave, let me just tell you one thing and I'll let you go because I know you're in a hurry. Jesus said to the religious leaders, "You are those who justify yourselves before men, but God knows your hearts; for that which is highly esteemed among men is an abomination in the sight of God" [Luke 16:15, author's paraphrase]. God's standard is one of holiness and utter moral perfection. That's what you have to face on judgment day, and that's why you need a Savior to wash away your sins and cleanse your heart—so God can extend his mercy toward you.

DAVE: That's all according to you.

RAY: Well, according to the Bible. I don't make this up.

DAVE: I don't care about the Bible. I don't believe in the Bible.

RAY: I know. I hope you'll think about what we talked about. Will you do that?

DAVE: I've done it many times. My opinion is everything in the universe is energy; everything will go back to [the] universe. If you want to see what happens after death, look at the squirrel when it's run over in the road—after it's been run over by a car. Watch it deteriorate, and eventually it goes down to nothing because all of its energy forces go back to energy.

RAY: Dave, you're going to get the shock of your death when you find that you pass on and stand in the presence of a holy God—and that's why you need Jesus to wash away your sins.

DAVE: And that's your opinion.

RAY: Thanks for talking to me.

DAVE: Oh, you're welcome.

Chapter 3

REAL GOD,
REAL JUDGMENT

"There are only two things in life that are sure: death and taxes." You've probably heard that saying before. It's a very common maxim, frequently attributed to Benjamin Franklin, who wrote to French scientist Jean-Baptiste Le Ray that "in this world, nothing is certain except death and taxes."[18]

However, the brilliant Mr. Franklin may have borrowed the phrase and forgotten to give attribution. It appeared more than six decades earlier in Daniel Defoe's *The Political History of the Devil*: "Things as certain as death and taxes, can be more firmly believ'd."[19] And it may be that Mr. Defoe *also* borrowed the phrase and forgot to give attribution. It seems it appeared in *The Cobler of Preston* by Christopher Bullock in 1716.[20]

Regardless of who first said it, I believe the adage needs a revision because it's just not true. My proposed edit is as follows: There are only two things in life that are sure: death and judgment day.

Plenty of people avoid taxes. No one will avoid death, and not a soul who dies in his or her sins will avoid the day of judgment.

HOW DOES A LOVING GOD JUDGE?

Of course, the world doesn't believe a judgment day is coming. A. W. Tozer once wrote,

> God's justice stands forever against the sinner in utter severity. The vague and tenuous hope that God is too kind to punish the ungodly has become a deadly opiate for the consciences of millions. It hushes their fears and allows them to practice all pleasant forms of iniquity while death draws every day nearer and the command to repent goes unregarded.[21]

People are never so illogical in their thinking as when they say that hell doesn't exist *because* they don't believe in it. Reality isn't determined by our beliefs. But there is an unseen root that feeds the weed of unbelief. Idolatry is the root. An erroneous image of God tells a person that the Almighty is too kind or too weak to judge the world. The following cynical question, which came to me by email one day, illustrates how we make a god in our own image:

> A simple question for you, Mr. Comfort. In your preaching, you tell everyone that they will stand before God to explain, etc. How much time does God allow for each interview? It would seem that as there are approximately 15 million deaths in the world each year [54 million], God would have only just over half a second for each interview. Or does he use "helpers" like Santa does?

That's a good question. How could this person's image of God possibly judge every human being for the crimes of murder, rape, lying, and stealing? Had this cynic known what the Scriptures reveal, he could have strengthened his argument. What he's really asking is how could God judge the complete thought life, every word and action of the billions of human beings who have lived and died throughout history? This includes all the secret deeds and those done in darkness (see Ecclesiastes 12:14). He's probably also wondering how his image of God possibly hears all the prayers of all the people in the world. These things are impossible, but with God we know that nothing is impossible (Luke 1:37). But unsaved people don't believe as God-fearers do: "The natural man does not receive the things of the Spirit of God, for they are foolishness to him; nor can he know them, because they are spiritually discerned" (1 Corinthians 2:14).

God is not natural. He is supernatural. He speaks, and creation comes into being. Not one atom in the universe exists without him. He can walk on water, give sight to the blind, multiply loaves and fishes, raise the dead, and, with his little finger, he can easily judge the world in righteousness. The apostle Paul alluded to this in his defense to King Agrippa:

> Now I stand and am judged for the hope of the promise made by God to our fathers. To this promise our twelve tribes, earnestly serving God night and day, hope to attain. For this hope's sake, King Agrippa, I am accused by the Jews. *Why should it be thought incredible by you that God raises the dead?* (Acts 26:6–8, emphasis added)

The resurrection of the dead is linked to the judgment of God, for Jesus himself said there is coming an hour when "all who are in the graves will hear His voice and come forth—those who have done good, to the resurrection of life, and those who have done evil, to the resurrection of condemnation" (John 5:28–29). If we insist on believing that God will not raise the dead and judge the world in righteousness, we open an ugly can of worms. We would then have to believe that God is unjust although the Bible is clear that he isn't. He gave every human being a conscience with an independent, accusing voice that would censure them when they violated his law (see Romans 2:15), but if there is no judgment day, God wouldn't have the will or the ability to enforce that law. That would make him a weak and evil judge. And that would be great news for wicked men and women because it would mean they need not fear God. It would mean the whole of humanity can give itself to every evil without any concern of impending judgment. It would mean that Jesus was wrong when he told us we should fear God because he has the ability to cast body and soul into hell. It would mean Jesus was lying. See how one untrue belief about God leads to another.

While such thoughts are repulsive, shallow, and unbiblical, they are clearly part of the world's philosophy, something we are warned to avoid: "Beware lest anyone cheat you through philosophy and empty deceit, according to the tradition of men, according to the basic principles of the world, and not according to Christ" (Colossians 2:8). The use of the word *beware* here is appropriate. Making up your own image of God based on this sinful world is a strong delusion. It is adult make-believe.

COMFORT OR TRUTH

When King Belshazzar finally trembled in fear at the sight of the writing on the wall, his faithful wife appeared and began to console him:

> The queen, because of the words of the king and his lords, came to the banquet hall. The queen spoke, saying, "O king, live forever! Do not let your thoughts trouble you, nor let your countenance change. There is a man in your kingdom in whom is the Spirit of the Holy God. And in the days of your father, light and understanding and wisdom…were found in him…Inasmuch as an excellent spirit, knowledge, understanding, interpreting dreams, solving riddles, and explaining enigmas were found in this Daniel, whom the king named Belteshazzar, now let Daniel be called, and he will give the interpretation." (Daniel 5:10–12)

The queen was aware of Daniel's godly reputation, and she believed he would bring a word of comfort to her terrified husband. Her faith was unwavering: "He will give the interpretation" (v. 12). She said, "O king, live forever! Do not let your thoughts trouble you, nor let your countenance change" (v. 10). But Daniel's interpretation wouldn't bring comfort; it would do just the opposite. It would reveal impending judgment. The king, therefore, was right to be troubled.

Ask most unbelievers what the Bible tells us about God, and they will take comfort in his goodness and love. But the Scriptures don't give impenitent sinners any consolation. Instead, the Bible warns that God's wrath remains on them (John 3:36) and that they are enemies of God in their evil thinking and wicked works (Colossians 1:21). Then ask unbelievers why God gave his law, and most will tell you that the Ten Commandments were given as rules to live by. They will even console themselves with words from the Sermon on the Mount, saying that Jesus gave us the Golden Rule (see Matthew 7:12), and that's their guide to life. They don't realize that the law sends out fiery wrath upon all those who have transgressed its holy precepts. The moral law is not something to be snuggled up to for consolation. Its purpose is to drive us toward mercy by helping us recognize how sinful we are in God's holy presence. It's only at the cross where we will find consolation.

The truth about God's judgment was not what Belshazzar expected to hear when Daniel was brought before him:

> I have heard of you, that the Spirit of God is
> in you, and that light and understanding and

excellent wisdom are found in you. Now the wise men, the astrologers, have been brought in before me, that they should read this writing and make known to me its interpretation, but they could not give the interpretation of the thing. And I have heard of you, that you can give interpretations and explain enigmas. Now if you can read the writing and make known to me its interpretation, you shall be clothed with purple and have a chain of gold around your neck, and shall be the third ruler in the kingdom. (Daniel 5:14–16)

Beware of all forms of flattery. I wonder how I would react if I were about to witness to someone, and before I began, they said they had heard of me and my good reputation—that God was with me and that light and understanding and excellent wisdom were found in me. I might be tempted to avoid speaking harsh things to someone who held me in such high esteem. I trust that my fear of God would stop me from speaking anything but the truth, as Daniel's own fear of the Lord did for him.

Our battle isn't against flesh and blood but against spiritual powers that often work in subtle ways (see Ephesians 6:12). The enemy would love for us to be friends with the world even though doing so makes us enemies of God (James 4:4). He wants us to compromise the words God has entrusted us to preach—to soften the message and not terrorize good people with archaic talk of the fear of the Lord. And the world will heap rewards on those who tickle ears with talk of anything other than sin, righteousness, and judgment. But Daniel would have none of it. He spoke uncompromising words of rebuke:

> Then Daniel answered, and said before the king, "Let your gifts be for yourself, and give your rewards to another; yet I will read the writing to the king, and make known to him the interpretation. O king, the Most High God gave Nebuchadnezzar your father a kingdom and majesty, glory and honor. And because of the majesty that He gave him, all peoples, nations, and languages trembled and feared before him. Whomever he wished, he executed; whomever he wished, he kept alive; whomever he wished, he set up; and whomever he wished, he put down. But when his heart was lifted up, and his spirit was hardened in pride, he was deposed from his kingly throne, and they took his glory from him. Then he was driven from the sons of men, his heart was made like the beasts, and his dwelling was with the wild donkeys. They fed

> him with grass like oxen, and his body was wet
> with the dew of heaven, till he knew that the
> Most High God rules in the kingdom of men,
> and appoints over it whomever He chooses."
> (Daniel 5:17–21)

Belshazzar's grandfather had not completely humbled himself before God. Pride is the stubborn taproot that must be destroyed with the axe of God's law because it often keeps sinners from approaching their Maker. Our unclean shoes must be removed because we stand on holy ground when we pray. The proud human heart must learn to kneel. Belshazzar knew all this, but he stiffened his neck. Scripture warns that a person who remains stubborn after being rebuked time and time again will suddenly be destroyed beyond all recovery (see Proverbs 29:1).

Daniel boldly named Belshazzar's sin of pride. He didn't gloss over it to maintain a peaceful relationship between him and Belshazzar:

> But you his son, Belshazzar, have not humbled
> your heart, although you knew all this. And
> you have lifted yourself up against the Lord of
> heaven. They have brought the vessels of His
> house before you, and you and your lords, your
> wives and your concubines, have drunk wine
> from them. And you have praised the gods of

silver and gold, bronze and iron, wood and stone, which do not see or hear or know; and the God who holds your breath in His hand and owns all your ways, you have not glorified. (Daniel 5:22–23)

It is only right that we glorify God. It is unethical to withhold any praise when it is due. We honor heroes and heap praise on great artists. We laud creative architects, skilled physicians, and record-breaking athletes. Sinful people will even glorify illicit sex, drug abuse, crime, drunkenness, and violence. But they refuse to glorify God. Jesus said that if we refused to glorify him, the stones would cry out in praise (Luke 19:40). Yet in their stubbornness and pride, sinful people have hearts harder than stone and will not give their Creator the praise due his name or show the slightest gratitude for the gift of life. In frustration, the psalmist pleads, "Oh, that men would give thanks to the LORD for His goodness, and for His wonderful works to the children of men!" (Psalm 107:21).

But when God, in his great mercy, opens our eyes to understand, we see his loving-kindness everywhere. It is then that praise spills from our lips as naturally as a song rises from a songbird in the fresh air of the early morning.

Daniel then gives the sinful king what he wanted to know but didn't want to hear:

"And this is the inscription that was written: MENE, MENE, TEKEL, UPHARSIN.

This is the interpretation of each word. MENE: God has numbered your kingdom, and finished it; TEKEL: You have been weighed in the balances, and found wanting; PERES: Your kingdom has been divided, and given to the Medes and Persians." Then Belshazzar gave the command, and they clothed Daniel with purple and put a chain of gold around his neck, and made a proclamation concerning him that he should be the third ruler in the kingdom. (Daniel 5:25–29)

Daniel passed the test. He proved faithful to his calling. He didn't back down for fear of the consequences that might come his way if he spoke the truth that Belshazzar's kingdom would fail. Like Nathan the prophet before him, he rebuked a king. What a betrayal it is to comfort sinners when they need rebuking. It is like placing a soft pillow under the sleeping head of a passenger who has to jump out of a plane. He doesn't need a pillow. He needs a parachute! But before he will put on that parachute, he must see his danger.

Those who fear God don't fear those around them—even if those people are kings, presidents, rich and powerful people, or bosses:

> I charge you therefore before God and the Lord Jesus Christ, who will judge the living and the dead at His appearing and His kingdom: Preach the word! Be ready in season and out of season. *Convince, rebuke, exhort, with all long-suffering and teaching.* For the time will come when they will not endure sound doctrine, but according to their own desires, because they have itching ears, they will heap up for themselves teachers; and they will turn their ears away from the truth, and be turned aside to fables. (2 Timothy 4:1–4, emphasis added)

The wonderful twist is that if we fear God now, we need not fear when we face him in judgment. We will have boldness on the day of wrath: "Love has been perfected among us in this: that we may have boldness in the day of judgment; because as He is, so are we in this world" (1 John 4:17).

SIGNS OF THE TIMES

After we remodeled our ministry building, we put a huge, new clock on the wall. However, even though the clock was large, from the other end of our packing room, it was very hard to see the time. This was because the hands were the same color as the clock face. For that reason, I later painted the hands white, and that fixed the problem. It was then easy to see the time at a glance.

Take a moment to consider the day in which we are living. Who could deny that we are getting close to the second coming of Christ? All of us should be paying attention to the prophetic time clock, now more than ever. Jesus rebuked his generation for not knowing the time in which they lived:

> Now as He drew near, He saw the city and wept over it, saying, "If you had known, even you, especially in this your day, the things that make for your peace! But now they are hidden from your eyes. For days will come upon you when your enemies will build an embankment around you, surround you and close you in on every side, and level you, and your children within you, to the ground; and they will not leave in you one stone upon another, because you did not know the time of your visitation." (Luke 19:41–44)

Pay attention to the signs of the times. Paint the hands on the clock white so the hour is evident. Knowing that the sky can roll back at any moment and that every mountain and island can be moved out of its place will help you to walk in the fear of the Lord.

The day of God's wrath will cause even the most prideful to run and hide. No one will be able to stand (Revelation 6:17). But God has warned us in his Word so that we might fear him today and be ready. Look at the fate of those who profess to be Christians but who fail to watch for his coming and don't, therefore, walk in the fear of the Lord:

> If that evil servant says in his heart, "My master is delaying his coming," and begins to beat his fellow servants, and to eat and drink with the drunkards, the master of that servant will come on a day when he is not looking for him and at an hour that he is not aware of, and will cut him in two and appoint him his portion with the hypocrites. There shall be weeping and gnashing of teeth. (Matthew 24:48–51)

Because the days are evil, we should redeem the time, telling every person we can that, because of God's great mercy, they may be counted perfectly righteous on the day all sin is punished. Being aware of the signs of the time helps increase our urgency to reach the unbelievers around us. It's not too late.

BACK TO THE MAKER

I've always been fascinated with drones. I wanted to purchase one that has a camera, but not knowing if I'd be able to fly the thing, I didn't want to pay too much. I found one online, and of course, I went straight to the one-star reviews to see what buyers didn't like about it. There were a number who said that it began flying well but that it suddenly got a mind of its own and disappeared into the heavens, never to be seen again. They couldn't even return it to get a refund. I jokingly wondered if the drone's makers had programmed it to return to them so they could resell it.

Every human being has been programmed to return to their Maker when they die. In speaking of that solemn moment, Solomon laments:

> For man goes to his eternal home,
> and the mourners go about the streets.
> Remember your Creator before the silver cord
> is loosed,
> or the golden bowl is broken,
> or the pitcher shattered at the fountain,
> or the wheel broken at the well.
> Then the dust will return to the earth as it was,
> and the spirit will return to God who gave it.
> (Ecclesiastes 12:5–7)

At death, every sinner has a terrifying appointment—a summons to face the judge of the universe and give an account for the evil they've committed. Of all the times we address God in our lifetime, it is before this frightening day that we need to make sure God hears our prayers. Without the law to show them the nature of sin, evil men and women will believe they are morally good and that all is well between them and heaven. But with the law comes a fear of the Lord that causes them to see their danger, depart from evil, and find life in Christ. How good it is that in him we are set free from guilt and fear! No longer do we run from the presence of the Lord and try to hide ourselves. No longer do we need to sow fig leaves together to cover the nakedness of our sin. We are justified by his amazing grace. We are clean in Christ and can face him without terror. I can recognize I am the chief of sinners and that my heart is evil, and smile in agreement when I see Jesus calling his beloved disciples evil: "If you then, being evil, know how to give good gifts to your children, how much more will your heavenly Father give the Holy Spirit to those who ask Him!" (Luke 11:13).

As God-fearing children, we each place our hand into the hand of our heavenly Father, knowing he will not lead us into temptation but will deliver us from evil. For his is the kingdom, the power and the glory, for ever and ever (see Matthew 6:13). And the more we trust him, the less we will be concerned with what the future may bring. We will no longer fear evil (see Psalm 23:4).

WITNESSING ENCOUNTER

The following interview was with an intimidating-looking man named Angel, who was about to go for a bike ride with a local church group. When I say that it was a church group, it may be more accurate to say that it was more like a social club (the members even tried to pull Angel away while I was sharing the gospel).

> RAY: What's the most important thing to you in life? Is it your own personal happiness? I mean, is that what you strive for above everything else?
>
> ANGEL: I strive to live a good life and try…try to lead by example.
>
> RAY: Do you believe the Bible when it says that our hearts are desperately wicked [Jeremiah 17:9]? Or do you think man is basically good?
>
> ANGEL: I honestly don't even need the Bible to see that. Right? I think men in general—meaning men and women—inherently we're bred with evil, right? We see it all the time growing up. Young kids that can be best friends growing up, could be teenagers and drift apart and

then start to hate each other for things that they never would've thought of as youngsters, right?

RAY: So, are you good or evil?

ANGEL: I'm human, right? So, I battle with trying not to be evil all the time. I try to do the right things. You yell at your kids; you have a bad day. When you cuss at people while you're driving—you're being evil, aren't you? But you're inherently fighting it all the time.

RAY: What's your standard?

ANGEL: So, what you try to do is be conscious of it. Be conscious of what you're doing.

RAY: But what's your standard?

ANGEL: What do you mean by *standard*?

RAY: Well, how do you gauge good and evil?

ANGEL: [SIGHS HEAVILY]

RAY: See, Hitler's evil [compared] to your evil would be different.

ANGEL: True, true. I get you. I think personally, I think what it is, is people that strive—right?—and consciously try to be good are not evil. People that thrive, prosper by being wicked and doing things that hurt other people or the world in general? That's evil to me.

RAY: Do you think God is happy with you or angry at you?

ANGEL: I think God is, uh, I think for the most part, happy with me.

RAY: He is?

ANGEL: I believe so.

RAY: So you don't believe what the Bible says?

ANGEL: Verbatim, no. And the reason is, I worked in printing for a long time, and—let's face it—the Bible is a book, when it comes down to the end of things. And yes, I'm sure at one point it was pure and it came from God, but what happens after? Unfortunately, men get ahold of things, don't they? And what do we do to things? We corrupt things constantly. Right? So, in doing so, I think some of the true meaning gets lost. And I think, politically, people in power at the time, thousands of years ago, control what ends up being put in that book that we're all reading.

RAY: You know, I've been reading the Bible every day without fail for forty-nine years. Never found a mistake in it. And I can find out by just looking on the internet if it's changed over the years. God's preserved his Word. You can trust it. Everything it says is truth. So, here's a question for you.

ANGEL: Okay.

RAY: On judgment day, how are you going to do? Are you going to make it to heaven?

ANGEL: When the time comes and God makes a decision on whether I go to heaven or hell, I'm going to heaven. No question about it.

RAY: Because you're a good person, basically.

ANGEL: I feel I am. I feel like I'm going to make it.

RAY: Okay, I'm going to challenge you on that. How many lies have you told in your life?

ANGEL: Countless.

RAY: Ever stolen something?

ANGEL: Yes.

RAY: Have you ever used God's name in vain?

ANGEL: Of course.

RAY: Would you use your mother's name as a cuss word?

ANGEL: No.

RAY: Why not?

ANGEL: I just wouldn't. And when I've used God's name and said, you know, heh, whatever the words are? You say that out of anger, right? You're not consciously thinking about it.

RAY: You know…what you're doing is substituting it for the word *s*—; you want to express disgust. Angel, that's called blasphemy—so serious it's punishable by death in the Old Testament. You'd never use your mother's name like that.

ANGEL: We have a bike ride with the church. I got to get going.

RAY: Give me, give me—

SOMEONE OFF CAMERA: All right, let's go, buddy!

ANGEL: I really got to go.

RAY (TO PERSON OFF CAMERA): Sir, can I share the gospel with him? Would you just give me two minutes? Please?

PERSON OFF CAMERA: These kids are going away, so—

RAY: Okay. Real, real quick.

ANGEL: Sure.

RAY: Angel, Jesus said if you look at a woman and lust for her, you commit adultery with her in your heart [Matthew 5:28]. So you've told me you're a lying, thieving, blasphemous adulterer at heart, and you have to face God on judgment day. If he judges you by the Ten Commandments, are you going to…

ANGEL: This is during my lifetime that all these things have happened, right?

RAY: Yes, absolutely.

ANGEL: So you ask for forgiveness, and you try to better yourself each and every day.

RAY: No, that won't work. I'll tell you why. If you stand in front of an earthly court, an earthly judge, and say, "Judge, I've violated the law, but I want to tell you—robbed the bank, shot the guard—but I'm improving my life. I've learned from these experiences. This happened over my life." He's going to say, "You're going to jail." So there's something else you need to be saved. Do you know what it is?

ANGEL: You're going to tell me.

RAY: It's God's mercy! If you're in court, and you've got no justification, you throw yourself on the mercy of the judge. And the Bible says God is rich in mercy to all that call upon him. He doesn't want you to end up in hell. He doesn't want to give you justice. And the reason he can show you mercy is that Jesus suffered and died on the cross for the sin of the world. Angel, we broke God's law; Jesus paid the fine. That's what happened on that cross. If you're in court—

ANGEL: We could discuss this a lot more, for a lot longer because I have some questions for you. Unfortunately, I got to get going.

RAY: I'll walk with you, just for a second because this is so important.

ANGEL: I have to ride, actually.

RAY: Okay, just let me finish the gospel if I may, because this is so important.

ANGEL: Okay. Sure.

RAY: Then Jesus rose from the dead and defeated death. Angel, if you're in court and someone pays your fine, the judge can legally let you off. He can say, "There's a stack of speeding fines here, but someone's paid them; you're free to go." And he can do that which is legal and right and just.

ANGEL: Mm-hmm.

RAY: And God can do that which is legal—he can let you live forever—because Jesus paid your fine in full. But what you must do is repent and trust alone in him. Angel, don't trust your goodness because it's not going to save you on judgment day. Trust in Jesus alone. You're like a man on the edge of a plane. He's going to jump ten thousand feet. This is his plan: doesn't have a parachute, but he's going to flap his arms. He's going to try and save himself. I'd say to that man, "Don't do that! Trust the parachute!" So transfer your trust from yourself to the Savior. And the second you do that, you've got God's promise he'll grant you forgiveness of sins and the gift of everlasting life. Is this making sense?

ANGEL: It does.

RAY: Thank you for staying. Everyone was saying, "Leave! Leave!"

ANGEL: [Laughs] I'll be able to catch them.

RAY: Will you think about what we talked about?

ANGEL: I sure will.

RAY: Do you have a Bible at home?

ANGEL: I do.

RAY: I noticed the group you're with actually prayed just before.

ANGEL: Correct. They're Greek Orthodox. They're neighbors.

RAY: And I prayed for you. I prayed for you before I met you, so please think about what we talked about, and have a sense of urgency. People get killed while riding bikes...

ANGEL: That's true.

Chapter 4

GUILTY, NOT CONDEMNED

There is a moment in the classic movie *Ben-Hur* when Judah's sister leans on loose roof tiling and it falls onto the Roman governor below. Each time I watch that scene, I whisper, "Noooo!" because I know the repercussions that will come from that one action. I do the same when I read about Adam and Eve's careless actions in the garden. As they lean toward sin, I recoil and say to myself, *Noooo! You have just brought utter ruin to the entire human race. You've opened wide the door to disease, pain, fear, loneliness, murder, rape, suicide, war, cruelty, terror, agony, hatred, depression, anguish, death, and horrifying damnation.* Every salty drop that has ever been shed into a massive ocean of tears can be traced back to this pivotal moment:

> The serpent said to the woman, "You certainly will not die! For God knows that on the day you eat from it your eyes will be opened [that is,

you will have greater awareness], and you will be like God, knowing [the difference between] good and evil." And when the woman saw that the tree was good for food, and that it was delightful to look at, and a tree to be desired in order to make one wise and insightful, she took some of its fruit and ate it; and she also gave some to her husband with her, and he ate. Then the eyes of the two of them were opened [that is, their awareness increased], and they knew that they were naked; and they fastened fig leaves together and made themselves coverings. (Genesis 3:4–7 AMP)

There are at least two ways we can react to the fall. We can get angry that we now inherit a sinful nature we didn't choose, along with endless suffering and then death—all from a sin that we didn't commit. Or we can stand back in holy fear that one transgression could have such frighteningly massive repercussions. The first reaction can make us bitter while the second can be beneficial—it can produce a lifelong fear of the Lord. As we encounter sin and the pain it produces in our everyday lives, we will have a continual reminder that God is holy and that sin always brings death:

Anyone who has rejected Moses' law dies without mercy on the testimony of two or three witnesses. Of how much worse punishment, do you suppose, will he be thought worthy who has trampled the Son of God underfoot, counted the blood of the covenant by which he was sanctified a common thing, and insulted the Spirit of grace? For we know Him who said, "Vengeance is Mine, I will repay," says the Lord. And again, "The LORD will judge His people." It is a fearful thing to fall into the hands of the living God. (Hebrews 10:28–31)

The fear of God will also hold back a sinful tongue that questions why he allowed the fall to happen—as though he was at fault or his judgments were unjust. As it says in Romans, "But indeed, O man, who are you to reply against God?" (Romans 9:20). Job opened his mouth without fearing the Lord as he should have, and he received a divine rebuke. We should take note:

Then the LORD answered Job out of the whirlwind, and said:

"Who is this who darkens counsel
by words without knowledge?
Now prepare yourself like a man;

I will question you, and you shall answer
Me." (Job 38:1–3)

God himself rebuked Job, and then asked him
a number of probing questions Job couldn't answer.
Job's response? "Behold, I am of little importance and
contemptible; what can I reply to You? I lay my hand
on my mouth" (40:4 AMP). Can you see what the fear
of the Lord does to humble and honest souls? It shows
them the truth. It gives them light to see that the earth
doesn't revolve around them. Until we see ourselves
as we truly are, we will think we are virtuous. The
"wretch" spoken of in John Newton's hymn "Amazing
Grace" doesn't sit well, and neither does owning
Adam's sin. Blaming Adam isn't a credible defense in
human courts, and it certainly won't be a defense on
judgment day.

In Romans, Paul also addressed the accusation
that God is somehow unfair in punishing us for the
sin of Adam:

> But the free gift is not like the offense. For if by
> the one man's offense many died, much more
> the grace of God and the gift by the grace of the
> one Man, Jesus Christ, abounded to many. And
> the gift is not like that which came through the
> one who sinned. For the judgment which came
> from one offense resulted in condemnation, but

the free gift which came from many offenses
resulted in justification. (5:15–16)

Look at what we have in Christ! Everlasting life
and pleasure forevermore. We have a glorious hope
in our death. What a fool I would be to question the
integrity of Almighty God when he has shown me
such kindness. No! I choose to fear the Lord. Without
godly fear, I would become bitter or angry when life
deals me a bad hand.

Job then humbled himself by asking a question he
knew didn't have an answer: "What shall I answer You?"
(Job 40:4). People with humble and honest hearts don't
have a comeback. Instead, they trust God's judgments.
In fear, they place a hand over their mouths and say, "I
am of little importance and worthy of contempt, but
God is the lover of my soul." Such self-awareness doesn't
glory in misery; it glories in the cross.

We are lifted up by the love and grace of God.
The wondrous cross on which the Prince of Glory
died is a continual pick-me-up. It is our focus. Both
now and forever. Because it is in that cross that we see
his love. We are guilty but not condemned. Paul rec-
ognized he was the chief of sinners (1 Timothy 1:15),
but he rejoiced in the richness of the mercy of God.
And we won't trust in that wonderful mercy without
the fear of the Lord: "In mercy and truth atonement is

provided for iniquity; and by the fear of the LORD one departs from evil" (Proverbs 16:6).

THE HUMAN PURSUIT OF JUSTICE

A day of judgment is coming; the Bible is consistent on this point (see Psalm 96:13; Isaiah 66:16; Daniel 7:9–10; Hebrews 9:27; 12:23; Revelation 6:15–17; 20:11–15). Common sense tells us that God must have an ultimate day of justice. Even humanity, with all its evil, will chase wicked criminals to the ends of the earth, spending millions of dollars to make sure they are punished for their crimes.

How grievous it is to know that many Nazis leaders escaped human justice for their depraved slaughter of millions of innocent people. One such case was that of Albert Speer. The Smithsonian Institute relates the frustrating story in an article titled "The Candor and Lies of Nazi Officer Albert Speer." He was Hitler's close friend and his minister of armaments. It was his duty to make sure the massive Nazi killing machine ran effectively. During the 1946 Nuremberg trials, Speer maintained he had no knowledge of even a single concentration camp, despite the fact that Germany maintained more than a thousand such facilities, including Auschwitz.

Speer was good-looking and eloquent, a gifted actor. While a number of his compatriots were sentenced to death, his sentence was just twenty years at Spandau Prison in Berlin, where he spent much of his time reading, all the while receiving free meals, lodging, and healthcare. He also "tended a garden and, against prison rules, wrote the notes for what would become best-selling books, including *Inside the Third Reich*."[22]

In 1966, after serving his sentence, Speer was released and became quite wealthy. He lived in a cottage in West Germany and cultivated an image of being a "good Nazi" who had spoken honestly about his past.

Speer was a close friend to one of history's evil-est human beings. He helped Hitler slaughter millions with great efficiency, but he got away with murder.

Then there was the case of Josef Mengele, a monster among Nazi monsters:

Mengele, in distinctive white gloves, supervised the selection of Auschwitz' incoming prisoners for either torturous labor or immediate exter-mination, shouting either "Right!" or "Left!" to direct them to their fate. Eager to advance his medical career by publishing "groundbreak-ing" work, he then began experimenting on live Jewish prisoners. In the guise of medical "treatment," Mengele injected, or ordered others to inject, thousands of inmates with everything from petrol to chloroform to study the chemicals' effects.[23]

Despite the many atrocities Josef Mengele committed, his crimes went unpunished according to human justice.

Albert Speer and Josef Mengele were not exceptions to the rule. Only a small fraction of Nazis were actually brought to justice:

> The number of suspects that have been brought to trial is a tiny percentage of the more than 200,000 perpetrators of Nazi-era crimes, said Mary Fulbrook, a professor of Germany History at University College London.
>
> "It's way too late," she told CNN of the latest trials. "The vast majority of perpetrators got away with it."
>
> In her new book, *Reckonings: Legacies of Nazi Persecution and the Quest for Justice*, Fulbrook says that of the 140,000 individuals brought to court between 1946 and 2005, only 6,656 ended in convictions.[24]

As shocking as that statistic is, it's important to remember that justice delayed is not always justice denied. The trial of these evil men for these unspeakably evil deeds can wait because nothing will be forgotten or overlooked by God. They, like all of us, will stand before God on judgment day. It may seem like an age for us—between the time that the Nazis committed these atrocities and when they stand before God—because we are prisoners of time. But God is not. Although God's timeline is different from ours, his judgment, in his time, will rectify the errors and injustice of human justice.

GOD'S DELAYED JUDGMENT

While many may believe God is unjust because he allows the wicked to flourish on earth today, Scripture tells us the wonderful reason why justice is delayed:

> Beloved, do not forget this one thing, that with the Lord one day is as a thousand years, and a thousand years as one day. The Lord is not slack concerning His promise, as some count slackness, but is longsuffering toward us, not willing that any should perish but that all should come to repentance. (2 Peter 3:8–9)

How foolish are those who believe that people don't have free will! The fact that God allows people to do evil is evidence of his kindness. He allowed us to lie, steal, lust, fornicate, commit adultery, and do all manner of evil *because of his mercy.* If he were not rich in mercy, we would all be struck down at the speed of lightning because of his love of justice. He has held back his wrath toward human beings not because he is slack in keeping his promise "as some count slackness, but [because he] is longsuffering toward us, not willing that any should perish but that all should come to repentance" (v. 9). How eternally grateful I am for such mercy! Had he come in judgment when I was a youth, I would have been damned justly. It is such a sobering thought and reminds me of the billions who are now as I was, not knowing what awaits them if they remain in their sins:

> The day of the Lord will come as a thief in the night, in which the heavens will pass away with a great noise, and the elements will melt with fervent heat; both the earth and the works that are in it will be burned up. Therefore, since all these things will be dissolved, what manner of persons ought you to be in holy conduct and godliness, looking for and hastening the coming of the day of God, because of which the heavens will be dissolved, being on fire, and the elements will melt with fervent heat? Nevertheless we, according to His promise, look for new heavens and a new earth in which righteousness dwells. (2 Peter 3:10–13)

And what is the essence of the message in much of the contemporary church? That God wants you to be a winner, that he's here for your marriage and your success. It's anything and everything *but* a warning motivated by what's to come. This is not as things should be! The Scriptures address skeptics who deny the coming judgment: "Scoffers will come in the last days, walking according to their own lusts, and saying, 'Where is the promise of His coming? For since the fathers fell asleep, all things continue as they were from the beginning of creation'" (vv. 3–4).

The people of Sodom received evidence that God was angry at their sin. Fire from heaven confirmed what their consciences had already told them. Noah's generation had the same evidence through water. May you and I believe the Word of God, just as Noah believed the warning of that which was to come (see Hebrews 11:7). May we also be moved out of our complacency by godly fear to warn everyone we meet so they, too, can trust in God's mercy— because that's what we will all need when the day of judgment arrives. Charles Spurgeon deeply cared for the unsaved, and his concern was never more evident than when he addressed the lost:

> What will ye do when the law comes in terror, when the trumpet of the archangel shall tear

you from your grave, when the eyes of God shall burn their way into your guilty soul, when the great books shall be opened, and all your sin and shame shall be published? Can you stand against an angry law in that day?[25]

The more people we warn about the coming judgment, the fewer who will realize only on judgment day that they should have had the fear of the Lord in their hearts their whole life. While we are all guilty of sin, Jesus' sacrifice on the cross opened the way for us to experience God's divine mercy. Only through this mercy can we stand in the presence of the only true God. Only through his mercy can we pray to a powerful, holy God—and know he listens.

WITNESSING ENCOUNTER

This couple was sitting in a car. Sean was sober, but Evelyn was extremely drunk. I thought she might be incoherent, but I was in for a surprise.

> RAY: So Sean—this is Evelyn over there, and she's had a little too much to drink, so she may be a little—
>
> EVELYN: No, I'm fine, I have not had too much to drink.
>
> SEAN: [Laughs] She's—she's had just a couple.
>
> RAY: Sean, is there an afterlife?

SEAN: I believe so.

RAY: Do you have a bucket list?

SEAN: Yes.

RAY: So, what do you want to do before you die?

SEAN: Everything. I want to drive a trophy truck.

RAY: What does that mean?

SEAN: It's an off-road vehicle that has, like, unlimited suspension and unlimited horsepower.

RAY: Where does that saying come from— "bucket list"?

SEAN: I have no idea.

RAY: I think it's from a movie that came out a number of years ago, called *The Bucket List*.

EVELYN: I love that movie.

SEAN: That's where it came from? It wasn't a saying before that?

RAY: Yeah, in a sense it was. It's from a book from many years ago where a man committed suicide; he hanged himself. He got on a bucket and kicked it. Yeah, so when someone "kicks the bucket," they die, and you've got a "bucket list." Are you afraid of death?

SEAN: No.

RAY: Come on, everyone's afraid of death.

SEAN: I'm not afraid of death. That's why I want to drive a trophy truck.

RAY: Do you have a death wish?

SEAN: Not a death wish, but I'm not afraid of death.

RAY: Let me put it another way. Do you love life?

SEAN: Of course.

RAY: It's sensible to be afraid of what can kill you, and death is called the grim reaper, and it's going to take your life. So, you should do everything you can to find out what death is and what you can do to counter it. Wouldn't that make sense?

SEAN: Sure.

RAY: There's a Bible verse that says, "The wages of sin is death" [Romans 6:23]. Have you ever heard that?

SEAN: I haven't. I'm not a church person.

RAY Death is what God pays you for your sins.

SEAN: Right.

RAY: Like a judge gives a criminal the death sentence. He says, "You've murdered three people. We're paying you in the death sentence. This is what you've earned; this is what you deserve, your wages." And sin is so serious to

God, he's given us capital punishment. That's the cause, according to the Bible. Do you think you're that bad, that God should put you to death for your sins?

SEAN: No. I think I'm a good person.

EVELYN: We're all going to die—but he's going to put you to death for your sins. But we're all going to die anyway, so what does that mean, like?

RAY: A girl was watching a sheep eat green grass, and she thought how nice and white the sheep looked against the green grass. Then it began to snow, and she thought how dirty the sheep looked against the white snow.

SEAN: Right.

RAY: Same sheep, different background. And when you and I compare ourselves to the background of man's standard, we come up reasonably clean. But when we compare ourselves to God's standard, the snowy-white righteousness of the Ten Commandments, it shows that we're not as clean as we thought.

SEAN: Right.

RAY: Make sense?

SEAN: Makes sense, yeah.

RAY: So, you think you're a good person?

SEAN: I do.

RAY: Okay, let's see how you do against God's law.

SEAN: Okay.

RAY: How many lies have you told in your life?

SEAN: Probably thousands.

Ray: What do you call someone who's told thousands of lies?

SEAN: Um, a liar.

RAY: What are you?

SEAN: I guess I'm a liar.

RAY: Do you still think you're a good person?

SEAN: I do.

RAY: Have you ever stolen something?

SEAN: Um, no. I don't steal.

RAY: Have you ever used God's name in vain? That's the third commandment.

EVELYN: What does that mean? Like saying, like—

SEAN: Like [blasphemy]. Yes, I have. Yes, I've said it, on accident.

RAY: Would you use your mother's name as a cuss word?

SEAN: No.

RAY: Tell me why not.

SEAN: Because—I just wouldn't.

RAY: Why not?

SEAN: Because it's not a normal thing.

RAY: Yeah, but you respect your mother. You wouldn't use her name in the place of a filth word to express disgust.

SEAN: Yeah, you're right. I don't know why we do that.

RAY: Hit your thumb with a hammer, you want to say something filthy, like the F-word, but instead you take God's holy name and use it in its place. It's called blasphemy, and there's a reason we do it. It's in John chapter seven, Jesus said, "The world hates me because I testify of its deeds that they're evil" [John 7:7, author's paraphrase]. And there's no greater evidence that we hate God than that we use his name as a cuss word. And yet, he gave us life. It's called blasphemy, and it's punishable by death in the Old Testament. Sean, I appreciate your honesty and your patience with me. Here's another one. This one will nail you to the wall. Do you still think you're a good person?

SEAN: Yeah. I still—yeah, I'm a great person.

RAY: I mean, morally good?

SEAN: Morally good.

RAY: Jesus said, "If you look at a woman and lust for her, you commit adultery with her in your heart" [Matthew 5:28, author's para-phrase]. Have you looked at a woman with lust?

SEAN: I guess I'm a—I'm an adulterer.

EVELYN: Yes, because he watches porn—

SEAN: I don't watch porn!

EVELYN: Yes, you do!

SEAN: No, I don't. No—

EVELYN: Yes, he does!

RAY: Have you had sex before marriage?

SEAN: No!

EVELYN: Really, babe?

SEAN: Never.

EVELYN: Are we married? Are we married right now? Are we married?

RAY: So, she's being like your conscience.

SEAN: Yes, she's being my conscience.

RAY: She's just telling the truth. So, Sean, now listen to this. This is the summation of your little court case. You've told me—and this is for you to judge yourself, okay? You've told me that you're a lying—and I can't believe you when you say that you've never stolen because you told me you're a liar—blaspheming, fornicating adulterer at heart. Do you still think you're a good person?

SEAN: I am a great person.

RAY: You know what you're doing?

SEAN: What am I doing?

RAY: You're adding self-righteousness to your sins.

SEAN: That's even worse, huh?

RAY: So, here's where we're going with this. If God judges you by the Ten Commandments on judgment day, we've looked at four—

SEAN: [Laughs] I guess I'm going to hell then, huh?

RAY: I trust you're laughing out of nervousness because that breaks my heart. Sean, I've just met you, but I love you. I care about you, and I'd hate for you to end up in hell.

SEAN: Well, I end up where I end up. I hope I'm going to heaven, but—

RAY: Well, it's not God's will that any perish [2 Peter 3:9]. The Bible says that. He has no pleasure in the death of the wicked [Ezekiel 33:11]. Tell me, what did God do for guilty sinners so we wouldn't have to end up in hell? Do you know?

EVELYN: He died for us on the cross.

RAY: He died for us on the cross.

EVELYN: And then he—like, for us to believe in him, and I believe that he—he was risen on the third day. I believe, I believe with all my life.

RAY: Let me talk to Sean for a minute. [To SEAN:] What she's saying is that Jesus died on the cross for our sins. Now, most people know that, but they don't know this. The Ten Commandments are called the moral law. You and I broke the law; Jesus paid the fine. Do you remember his last words on the cross?

SEAN: No.

RAY: Just before he dismissed his Spirit, he said, "It is finished" [John 19:30]. Why do you think he said that?

SEAN: I have no idea. Like I said, I'm not a church-going person. I am today. I started today.

RAY: Well, you and I broke God's law. Jesus paid the fine. And when he was saying, "It is finished," he was saying the debt has been paid. Sean, if you're in court and someone pays your fine, the judge can let you go even though you're guilty. He can say, "Sean, there's a stack of speeding fines. This is real serious, but someone's paid them. You're out of here." And he can do that which is legal and right and just. Even though you're guilty, you walk because someone paid your fine.

And even though you and I are guilty before God of heinous crimes in his sight, he can let us live forever. He can take the death sentence off us because Jesus paid the fine in his life's blood, rose again on the third day, and if you'll simply repent of sin—turn from sin, and trust in Jesus, like you'd trust a parachute—you have a promise from the God that cannot lie: he'll forgive your sins and grant you everlasting life. The reason God can't lie is because he's without sin. The Bible says it's impossible for God to lie. That means, when he says, "I'll forgive your sins and grant you everlasting life as a free gift," you can bank on it. You can rest on it; you can trust it because he's faithful. Is this making sense?

SEAN: Yes. It makes me feel a little better.

RAY: Well, if a doctor tells you you've got a terminal disease, and you freak out when you see you've got the symptoms, that's scary. But if he says, "Hey, I've got a cure in my pocket," then it makes sense. And I've tried to give you the cure in the gospel. Death is your disease; sin is the disease, and the cure is trust in Jesus. Are you going to think about what we talked about?

SEAN: I sure will. I learned a little bit today.

RAY: A little bit?

SEAN: I learned a lot.

RAY: Do you have a Bible at home?

SEAN: I don't.

RAY: Can I give you a publication we put out called *The Bible's Four Gospels*?[26]

SEAN: Sure.

RAY: Will you read it?

SEAN: I will.

RAY: I'm so encouraged that you're listening, and I do hope that you'll really think about it, and I'd like you to think about it with this sense of sobriety: you could die tonight.

SEAN: I could.

RAY: One hundred and fifty thousand people die every twenty-four hours, so this is deadly serious. And I want to ask you one more question before we cease. Would you sell one of your eyes for a million dollars?

SEAN: No.

RAY: Would you sell both for a hundred million?

SEAN: Nope. I like my vision.

RAY: And yet your eyes are merely the windows of your soul. The real Sean looks out these windows. So, if your eyes are without price, how much is your soul worth? Jesus said,

"What shall it profit a man if he gains the whole world, and yet loses his own soul?" [Mark 8:36, author's paraphrase]. So, that's the sense of sobriety I want you to think about it with. How precious your life is, and how it could be taken from you in an instant, and you find yourself in death in your sins, heading for hell. That'd be horrific, so are you going to think about it with that sense of sobriety?

SEAN: I sure will. Definitely.

RAY: Let me get you that *The Bible's Four Gospels*, okay?

SEAN: Thank you. I appreciate it.

[A FEW MINUTES LATER]

RAY: So, what were you just saying?

SEAN: She just went to a Christian church for the first time today.

RAY: Today?

SEAN: Yes.

RAY: Did you go with her?

SEAN: I did.

RAY: So, this is kind of strange that suddenly I come along and share the gospel.

SEAN: It was kind of strange that you showed up today and started telling us that.

Chapter 5

SCRIPTURE REVEALS

There are certain parts of the Bible that put a healthy fear of God in my heart. I shudder when I read them. These passages can be among the bitterest of pills to swallow, but studying them can have a great health benefit; they can even be a comfort if we understand all that is at stake in the choices we make.

Of course, when we think of the comfort of the Scriptures, we tend to think of consoling verses like Isaiah 26:3, where God promises perfect peace to those whose minds are stayed on him. But frightening verses can also give us comfort. A little child who sits on his father's knee and sees bulging biceps can take as much comfort in his strength as he does in his gentle voice.

In the opening chapter of the book of Proverbs, God appeals to sinners with a sobering rebuke in the form of a promise. He assures sinners that if they will turn from their sin, he will "surely" pour out his Spirit on them and make his words known (v. 23).

We are like Adam in Genesis 3—hiding because of our guilt and, all the while, loving that which is evil. Conscience whispers as we indulge in our unbridled lusts. Oh, how we once ran like a raging stallion toward the pleasures of sin, but God kept his promise; he made his words known to us through the gospel. We had the same response that Lazarus had when Jesus raised him from the dead. Jesus put life in his body, but Lazarus had to obey Jesus' command to come out of the tomb. He wasn't pulled by Jesus from the grave. He could have stayed in the cold and dark sepulcher, but he heard the voice of the Son of God, stood to his feet, and went to Jesus. But there is a terrifying fate awaiting those who hear the same voice but stiffen their necks and harden their hearts:

> Turn at my rebuke;
> surely I will pour out my spirit on you;
> I will make my words known to you.
> Because I have called and you refused,
> I have stretched out my hand and no one regarded,
> because you disdained all my counsel,
> and would have none of my rebuke,
> I also will laugh at your calamity;

I will mock when your terror comes,
when your terror comes like a storm,
and your destruction comes like a whirlwind,
when distress and anguish come upon you.
"Then they will call on me, but I will not answer;
they will seek me diligently, but they will not
find me.
Because they hated knowledge
and did not choose the fear of the LORD."
(Proverbs 1:23–29)

This portion of Scripture doesn't describe the easy-
going God we hear preached from many pulpits these
days. But it isn't an isolated or obscure passage, where
the supposed wrath-filled "God of the Old Testament"
vents his anger. Speaking of the fear of the Lord as
revealed in Scripture, A. W. Tozer said,

> We have but to read the Scriptures with our
> eyes open and we can see this truth running
> like a strong cable from Genesis to Revelation.
> The presence of the divine always brought fear
> to the hearts of sinful men. Always there was
> about any manifestation of God something
> that dismayed the onlookers, that daunted and
> overawed them, that struck them with a terror
> more than natural. This terror had no relation
> to mere fear of bodily harm. It was a dread

consternation experienced far in toward the center and core of the nature, much farther in than that fear experienced as a normal result of the instinct for physical self-preservation.[27]

There is no change in God's character from Genesis to Revelation, and so our need to fear the Lord does not change either. In the New Testament, he threatens the same judgments on "those who are self-seeking and do not obey the truth, but obey unrighteousness—indignation and wrath, tribulation and anguish, on every soul of man who does evil" (Romans 2:8–9). When I read these passages, I must do so in light of the bright mercy of the cross. God's wrath may loom large, but his free gift of salvation looms larger still.

SCRIPTURE REVEALS SIN

When the Ten Commandments are used to show sinners their sin, God's law becomes a lighthouse in a storm of evil, its brilliant beam revealing treacherous rocks:

> We know that the law is good if one uses it lawfully, knowing this: that the law is not made for a righteous person, but for the lawless and insubordinate, for the ungodly and for sinners, for the unholy and profane, for murderers of fathers and murderers of mothers, for

manslayers, for fornicators, for sodomites, for
kidnappers, for liars, for perjurers, and if there
is any other thing that is contrary to sound
doctrine, according to the glorious gospel of the
blessed God which was committed to my trust.
(1 Timothy 1:8–11)

When people shake off the fear of God, they
unwittingly unleash a beast that easily overcomes
them. The Bible says that in the face of a loose woman,
a sinful man is defenseless: "For by means of a harlot
a man is reduced to a crust of bread; and an adulteress
will prey upon his precious life" (Proverbs 6:26).

The "beast" isn't the loose woman. She just
brings the beast out of its cave. The beast is our
propensity for sin. My heart breaks for people who
love their spouse but love sin even more. They melt
like butter under the heat of lust. Sin deceives them
because it has a deceptive glamour, and it unleashes a
monster that will devour their once-happy marriage.
They don't understand the power of the evil that sits
in their hearts: "The way of the wicked is like darkness; they do not know what makes them stumble"
(Proverbs 4:19).

Only a fool ignores signs that say "Poison!"
"Keep back!" "Do not enter!" "Danger!" or "High volt-
age!" Scripture offers us a graveyard filled with those

who ignored such warnings and suffered the consequences, such as this passage from Proverbs:

> My son, pay attention to my wisdom;
> lend your ear to my understanding,
> that you may preserve discretion,
> and your lips may keep knowledge.
> For the lips of an immoral woman drip honey,
> and her mouth is smoother than oil;
> but in the end she is bitter as wormwood,
> sharp as a two-edged sword.
> Her feet go down to death,
> her steps lay hold of hell. (Proverbs 5:1–5)

As we have seen, we human beings are easily
ensnared by sin. Our heads are easily turned by whispers from the world, the flesh, and the devil. However,
God has provided for us his Word so that we can
remind ourselves daily about the warnings against sin
and blessings for those who fear him.

SCRIPTURE REVEALS GOD'S TRUE NATURE

It's to our advantage to know the power of water,
fire, and gravity. Water preserves our life, fire gives
us warmth, and gravity keeps our feet safely on the
ground. But at the same time, each of these can kill
us. We learn not to breathe in water or to be too close
to the heat of an open fire or to test the law of gravity

when we're standing near the edge of a cliff. Some don't have any choice. They lose their lives because of flash floods, tsunamis, wildfires, or a fall from a great height due to someone else's negligence or cruelty. But there is one choice we do have—the choice to fear the Lord. It's a decision that will always be to our advantage in this life and into the next.

That's why we should treasure, above fine gold, the Scripture passages that give us knowledge of God. Are we filled with fear as we read the Holy Scriptures? Do we pore over every word with godly fear, or do we ignore it or even skim-read it as we would a cheap novel? If we have the fear of God in us, we will believe the Bible's promised blessings and its threatening judgments, and we will be drawn to God's mercy like a moth to a flame. If gold was your only means of survival in a famine (because it gave you bargaining power to get food for your family), you would do everything you could to make sure it wasn't stolen. So be wise and make sure you don't let the enemy steal your fear of the Lord. Don't entertain wrong thoughts about the nature of God.

The image of a God who smiles at sin, whose patience is infinite and inexhaustible, only exists in the minds of those who lack the fear of the Lord. They choose to ignore the knowledge of God given to us in Holy Scripture. It is just as God tells us in Proverbs:

"They hated knowledge and did not choose the fear of the LORD" (1:29). But if we read the Scriptures carefully, we will see that the fear of the Lord routinely accompanied divine visitation. Rarely did any person have fellowship with God without first falling on their face, trembling, or crying, "Woe is me. I'm undone!" Observing this, the puritan John Bunyan wrote:

> Man crumbles to dust at the presence of God; yea, though he shows himself to us in his robes of salvation. We have read how dreadful and how terrible even the presence of angels have been unto men, and that when they have brought them good tidings from heaven (Judg 13:22; Matt 28:4; Mark 16:5, 6). Now, if angels, which are but creatures, are, through the glory that God has put upon them, so fearful and terrible in their appearance to men, how much more dreadful and terrible must God himself be to us, who are but dust and ashes![28]

God has power greater than the human mind can comprehend, but this fact is often overlooked today. Consider the following dilemma one Christian has because Scripture doesn't paint a picture of the congenial God he's imagined exists. Here's a message I once received:

Ray, I am a real Christian. Something awful happened! I found maybe fault in the Bible. First, I read in the Old Testament that a woman was to be stoned to death for having sex before marriage, for lying about not being a virgin. This is awful. And how do you explain a man being put to death for one mess up with sex? Also, I read in Matthew 15:4: "For God commanded, saying, Honour thy father and mother: and, he that curseth father or mother, let him die the death" [KJV]. Then, contradicting that, Jesus says that no one may be his disciple unless they hate their own father and mother. Luke 14:26 [says], "If any man come to me and hate not his father, and mother, and wife, and children, and brethren, and sisters, yea, and his own life also, he cannot be my disciple" [KJV]. Ray, please, has the devil or demons or evil somehow distorted God's words for me right now? Why did I read this stuff this way? Then I read more and found more…I think some evil is trying to distort God's truth for me. Please can you make sense of this?

He, too, was finding parts of the Bible that made him shudder. I replied:

John, that same unbending and merciless law will judge the world on judgment day. Jesus warned that it will be so fearful, it will be like a stone that grinds people to powder (Luke 20:18). When something is ground to powder, it is done. Nothing is left. On judgment day, God's full fury will fall on sinners, just as it did on the guilty in the Old Testament. That's why they need the Savior. That's why I plead with the lost. Hope that helps.

It's crucial that every human being comes to understand the truth about God's righteous judgments. In summing up the meaning of life, the book of Ecclesiastes puts the issue front and center:

> Let us hear the conclusion of the whole matter:
>> Fear God and keep His commandments,
>> for this is man's all.
>> For God will bring every work into judgment,
>> including every secret thing,
>> whether good or evil. (Ecclesiastes 12:13–14)

The culmination of Solomon's wisdom came to a point in a warning we all need to hear: *every* work will be judged. Without these uncomfortable passages of Scripture, we wouldn't have a lamp to our feet and a light for our path. We would be in the darkness, unaware of the dangers that lay ahead:

> My people are destroyed for lack of knowledge.
> because you have rejected knowledge,
> I also will reject you from being priest for Me;
> because you have forgotten the law of your God,
> I also will forget your children. (Hosea 4:6)

The knowledge we garner from the Bible (particularly from God's moral law) should leave us with the healthy conviction that God can destroy both body and soul in hell.

SCRIPTURE REVEALS OUR TRUE REFLECTION

The average person glances in the mirror multiple times a day. We do that not just because we are vain but to make sure everything is publicly acceptable. There are man-made mirrors, and there are natural mirrors, such as calm water. Both reflections can show us what we look like, but neither is truly accurate because they can only show us a reverse image of reality. However, the law of God gives us a perfect reflection:

> Be doers of the word, and not hearers only, deceiving yourselves. For if anyone is a hearer of the word and not a doer, he is like a man

observing his natural face in a mirror; for he observes himself, goes away, and immediately forgets what kind of man he was. But he who looks into the perfect law of liberty and continues in it, and is not a forgetful hearer but a doer of the work, this one will be blessed in what he does. (James 1:22–25)

Prayer is one of the ways we become doers of the Word. I'm not great when it comes to prayer. Some have a real gift. I don't. I struggle with words and with commitment. One of my problems is a wandering mind, so I have to pray with resolve. I *make* myself pray. For thirty-eight years, I got up most nights around midnight to pray, but as I aged, I found that sleep would overtake me. After I turned seventy, I stopped getting up. Instead, I prayed at night in bed, which helped. I also developed the mentality to "pray without ceasing" as 1 Thessalonians 5:17 calls me to do. Whenever I'm alone, I try and remember to pray— because prayer is my oxygen. Without it, I would lack spiritual energy, then I will die. While it's important that I pray, it's just as important to make sure my prayers are heard. Therefore, I never approach the Lord without having a pure conscience, one that is void of offense toward God. And I can have this instantly by making a simple confession of any sin (such as bad attitudes or selfishness) Scripture reveals in my life and having trust in the righteousness of Christ.

Developing a pure conscience is why we look into the Scriptures daily with a healthy fear of God, always reflecting on what our thoughts and actions look like in the light of his Word. If you want to be doers of the Word, you have to ask yourself: *Are you chasing after sinful desires? Or are you studying Scriptures to develop an accurate view of God and a fear of the Lord that leads toward obedience?*

WITNESSING ENCOUNTER

The following transcript is from a video in which a likable young lady professed her atheism.

> RAY: What are your thoughts on the afterlife?
>
> GABBY: I personally think that we die, and our body is used to, you know, revive the earth, and that's it. Our spirits doesn't go anywhere. I don't really believe that we have spirits, just consciousness.
>
> RAY: Do you think you have a soul?
>
> GABBY: No, but I do believe that, you know, you should be a good person and that just because you don't have a soul there, you know, that we should all live in chaos and that there's no reason to treat people well, you know.

RAY: Let me see if I can change your mind about the soul thing.

GABBY: Okay.

RAY: Do you know the Bible uses the word *life* and *soul* synonymously? They're the same thing. The life and the soul.

GABBY: Mm-hmm.

RAY: Your name's Gabby. The real Gabby is looking out your eyes…

GABBY: Mm-hmm.

RAY: …and speaking to me through your mouth. It's your soul, your life. You believe in God, but you don't believe in human institutions?

GABBY: I don't believe in God.

RAY: Let me see if I can change your mind about that.

GABBY: Okay.

RAY: I'm gonna give you some information. First, let me tell you a little story. A man got on a bus. He was completely blind. Someone on the bus stood up and gave him his seat. Was that a good thing to do?

GABBY: The man that got on the bus was blind, and somebody gave him his seat? Yes, that would be a good thing to do. Yes.

RAY: You know, it wasn't. It was a really bad thing to do. You know why?

GABBY: Why?

RAY: It was the bus driver who gave up his seat.

GABBY: [Laughs]

RAY: Now, this is not a joke. It illustrates something very important. It shows that information can change our mind.

GABBY: Yes.

RAY: Completely.

GABBY: That's true.

RAY: You did a complete reversal. "That was a good thing to do." No, it wasn't! It was bad.

GABBY: Yes. [Laugh]

RAY: So I'm going to try and give you information so you can make a one-eighty...

GABBY: Mm-hmm.

RAY: ...around about regarding the existence of God. This is what somebody believes who believes there's no God: they believe the scientific impossibility that nothing created everything—flowers and birds and trees, the sun, the moon, the stars, the seasons.

GABBY: That it just happened.

RAY: No, not just happened, but nothing was the creative force.

GABBY: Okay.

RAY: They don't believe there was nothing in the beginning.

GABBY: Mm-hmm.

RAY: They believe it was nothing that made everything.

GABBY: Mm-hmm.

RAY: Because that's what we default to. Either there was a Creator of some sort, an intelligent designer that made eyes and flowers and the hummingbird and puppies, or it all just happened, because nothing created it. So would I be right in saying you just don't know if God exists, rather than…

GABBY: I just don't know. If I were, you know, if I were shown some kind of evidence, sure, I would change my mind. But at this point I've never had any feeling that—or any visual evidence that—there is a God, only…just disappointment. I mean, my life isn't terrible or anything, but you see so much tragedy around you, it's hard to believe that someone with control wouldn't help, you know.

RAY: Okay. Let me come back to the tragedy thing and see if I can give you evidence for God's existence.

GABBY: Uh-huh.

RAY: When you look at a car, how do you know there was a car manufacturer, that someone made it?

GABBY: Uhh, because it's got a brand name on it, and their company has a reputation, I guess.

RAY: Let's say there was no brand name on your car. Would you think it happened by accident?

GABBY: No.

RAY: No.

GABBY: I had to buy it from somebody.

RAY: You know that…

GABBY: Yes.

RAY: …it was designed because…

GABBY: Yes.

RAY: …it has design. And when you look at a building, you know there was a builder, even if the builder died two hundred years ago. You know there was a builder because buildings don't build themselves.

GABBY: Yes.

RAY: So when you look at a painting, you know there was a painter, even if the painter died three hundred years ago.

GABBY: Yeah.

RAY: You know there was a painter because paintings don't paint themselves. So when you look at the seasons and the flowers and the birds—let's just do a little pan here—the blueness of the sky and the sun and how it comes up on time every day, we can predict the sunrise a hundred years hence because there's such order. And there's order from the atom through the universe in everything you look at. So creation is evidence of a Creator. In fact, when we [the United States] left Great Britain through the…through independence from Britain, we created what was called the Declaration of Independence.

GABBY: Mm-hmm.

RAY: It wasn't just that…We didn't say to Britain, "Hey, we're thinking of parting from you guys." No, it was a declaration: "This is what's happening." And the Bible says, "The heavens declare the glory of God" [Psalm 19:1]. Every time you look at the painting of the sky—those magnificent clouds that give us rain, that give us life—we look at a sunrise or a sunset, all these things show us that God exists. But we don't feel comfortable because we know that God demands moral responsibility. Second thought: you said suffering is evidence against God's existence. Human suffering is everywhere we look. But human suffering shouldn't be used as evidence to reject God and the Bible but very real evidence to accept it because the Bible says we live in a fallen creation with disease, pain, suffering, and death. So the Bible gives the explanation for all these things. So that should substantiate your faith in God, not destroy it. So, you said earlier on, you're a good person.

GABBY: Yes, I mean, I try to live, uh…I try to treat people the way that I would want to be treated, yes.

RAY: So…

GABBY: Yes.

RAY: …what's the standard you live by?

GABBY: Only affecting people in a positive way. You know, uh, try to make a good difference, if any. Or, you know, just try to take care of yourself and the people around you.

RAY: What about the Ten Commandments? Would they be a good standard to live by? You shall not steal, you shall not lie, you shall not commit adultery, you shall not kill [Exodus 20:13–16].

GABBY: Umm…yes, uh…for the most part, yeah, you shouldn't do other things that affect people in a negative way. I mean, feelings—sometimes you can't help but hurt people's feelings, I guess, but that's a little bit different. Those are subjective. It's not the same as if I physically were to hurt you or something. You know what I mean? Um…

RAY: So I'm going to give you a standard to judge yourself by. So this is for you, not for me.

GABBY: Okay.

RAY: Are you ready?

GABBY: Yes.

RAY: Can you be honest with me?

GABBY: Sure.

RAY: How many lies have you told in your life?

GABBY: I lie every day. [Laughs]

RAY: What do you call someone who lies every day?

GABBY: A liar? I don't know.

RAY: Yes, you do.

GABBY: Yes.

RAY: That's right. Have you ever stolen something?

GABBY: No.

RAY: Is this one of those lies you tell every day?

GABBY: Uhh…you know? Uhh…well, I should say, what constitutes stealing something? Because if you borrow it from family or something like that, it's different.

RAY: Well, when you borrow it from a bank and you don't return it.

GABBY: No, that is stealing. Yeah, stealing's bad. [Laughs]

RAY: Or you download music off the internet, and it's not yours.

GABBY: Oh, I've done that. [Laughs]

RAY: Yes…that's theft. Still think you're a good person?

GABBY: Yes.

RAY: Ever use God's name in vain?

GABBY: I literally just did during this interview.

RAY: Yes.

GABBY: And I'm so sorry if it was offensive. [Laughs]

RAY: I caught it.

GABBY: Yes.

RAY: But I held onto it, to remind you of something.

GABBY: [Laughs]

RAY: Would you ever use your mother's name as a cuss word?

GABBY: Um, no. [Laughs]

RAY: Tell me why not?

GABBY: Umm, it doesn't have the same weight as if I were to just blurt, "Renée."

RAY: You wouldn't use your mom's name as a cuss word because…

GABBY: No!

RAY: …that's such a horrible thing to do. Instead of using a filth word beginning with *s* to express disgust, to use her name in its place would be horrible. And yet that's what you've done with God's holy name; you've substituted it for a filth word.

GABBY: Yes.

RAY: The God that gave you your mother and your eyes and life itself. It's called blasphemy.

GABBY: Yes.

RAY: Very serious in God's eyes. So serious it's punishable by death in the Old Testament. Little personal here—Jesus said, if you look with lust, you commit adultery in the heart [Matthew 5:28]. Have you ever looked with lust?

GABBY: Sure. Yes.

RAY: So, I'm not judging you, Gabby, but you've just told me you're a lying, thieving, blasphemous…

GABBY: [Laughs] I'm a sinner!

RAY: …adulterer at heart, and you have to face God on judgment day. So this is where we're heading with this: If God judges you by the Ten Commandments—we looked at four—are you gonna be innocent or guilty?

GABBY: If you're going send me to hell, then I guess that's what I get, you know?

RAY: Oh, boy! I would hate that to happen. Do you know what death actually is? Do you know the biblical definition of *death*?

GABBY: What is it?

RAY: It's wages. Did you know that?

GABBY: I've never heard that.

RAY: Yes, it's a famous Bible verse. "The wages of sin is death" [Romans 6:23]. God's paying you in death for your sins. It's like a judge has a heinous criminal that's, uh, raped three girls and murdered them. The judge says, "You've earned the death sentence. This is what's due to you. This is your wages. We're gonna pay you in the death sentence." And sin is so serious to a holy God, he's paying you in death for sin. He's given you capital punishment. And if you die in your sins, God will justly damn you. Do you know what *mens rea* is?

GABBY: What is it?

RAY: It's a legal term. It means a criminal must have knowledge that what he did was wrong or you can't prosecute him.

GABBY: Oh, okay.

RAY: If he did something but he didn't know it was wrong, you can't prosecute him. And we're guilty before God because God gave us a conscience. None of us can say, "I didn't know it was wrong to lie, steal, fornicate, lust, blaspheme."

GABBY: Yes.

RAY: We've got this inner knowledge, this judge on the courtroom in the mind that accuses us when we do wrong. So here's the big question: Does it concern you that if you died today and you were guilty before God, you'd end up damned in hell?

GABBY: No, because what would I do to change it? What can I do right now to change it?

RAY: Well, you can do something because of what God has done. Do you know what God has done?

GABBY: Uhh…what is that?

RAY: Jesus died on the cross for the sin of the world. You've heard that?

GABBY: But…yes, but does that mean that I could just go to church and be okay now? Or…

RAY: No, not at all.

GABBY: Oh. Then what is it?

RAY: Let me share the gospel with you and get your thoughts.

GABBY: Okay.

RAY: The Ten Commandments are called the moral law. You and I broke the law; Jesus paid the fine. That's what happened on the cross. That's why he said just before he died—just before he dismissed his spirit—he said three very profound words. He said, "It is finished" [John 19:30]. That's a weird thing to say when you're dying—"It is finished." But he was saying the debt has been paid. We broke God's law; Jesus paid the fine. Gabby, if you're in court and someone pays your fine, a judge can legally let you go. He can say, "Gabby, there's a stack of speeding fines here—this is deadly serious—but someone's paid 'em. You're free to go." And even though you're guilty, he can let you walk because someone paid your fine. And even though you and I are guilty of crimes worthy of death, worthy of damnation, God can let us go because Jesus paid the fine on the cross. He can do that which is legal and yet show us mercy and forgive us and let us walk, take the death sentence off us.

GABBY: So what do we do?

RAY: That is the greatest question you'll ever ask: "What should I do?" And the Bible says—because Jesus then rose from the dead and defeated death—that God can grant you everlasting life as a free gift. And if you'll simply repent of your sins and trust in Jesus, like you trust a parachute, you've got God's promise—and it's impossible for God to lie—that he'll grant you everlasting life as a free gift. If you're on a plane ten thousand feet up, and you didn't have a parachute on, why would you put on a parachute?

GABBY: To save yourself? From dying?

RAY: Yes, you see a danger.

GABBY: Yes.

RAY: Fear is your friend, not your enemy, in that case.

GABBY: Okay.

RAY: And so what I've tried to do, because I care about you, is put the fear of God into you. Because fear is your friend in this point, not your enemy.

GABBY: Yes.

RAY: Fear of God is the beginning of wisdom [Proverbs 9:10]. If it caused you to put on a parachute before you jump, it's doing you a favor. And if you put on the Lord Jesus Christ because you're afraid of death and hell and God's justice, that's a good motive.

GABBY: So what you're saying…all I need to do is repent for my sins and then try to continue to not sin, and if I do, then go back and repent some more, and then I'll be okay?

RAY: Well, you're trusting in Christ. He will forgive you, once and for all. And if you do something that you know is morally wrong, you just say, "God, please forgive me." And the Bible says, "If we confess our sins, He is faithful and just to forgive us our sins and to cleanse us from all unrighteous" [1 John 1:9]. So it's like if you… when you're a little kid, your dad gives you a bath, and you get dirty, you just wash yourself again.

GABBY: Wow! That's a nice way to put it. [Laughs]

RAY: Yes! So God says he'll clean you of sin so you're free from his wrath on judgment day, and he's made the way for you to be clean continually by just saying, "Lord, please forgive me. I did something wrong. I lost my temper, I looked at something I shouldn't have looked at, and I'm feeling bad about it. Please forgive me." And the Bible says that's contrition or being sorry for your sins. One last illustration: a man who was rich fell into the ocean, and he started drowning because he was wearing a belt that weighed forty pounds. It was full of gold. He wouldn't take it off because he loved his money, and it took him to his death. And there's one thing that'll drag you to hell—it's your love for sin. And what you've gotta do is say, "God, I'm gonna turn from sin. I'm not gonna play the hypocrite. I'm gonna repent and trust in Jesus and trust in your mercy." And Gabby, I wouldn't lie to you. This is such an important issue. This is your eternal life we're talking about. This is the salvation of your soul. So, will you think about what we talked about today?

GABBY: All the time! I'm sure I will think about it all the time! [Laughs]

RAY: Okay.

GABBY: I've thought about this a lot…you know, I have a lot of friends and family that are pretty religious and believe in God and…

RAY: They're Christians?

GABBY: Christians or other religions. My stepmom's Catholic, and I grew up occasionally going to Catholic church with her, um, and then also going to a Christian youth group, on my own, all through grade school. But I feel…I almost feel like, for me personally, I envy people that do believe in God and do believe in an afterlife because it's really scary to think about dying and just becoming nothingness. It is really scary. And I feel like people that believe in a beautiful afterlife that they deserve to be at, uh, I feel like they have some kind of peace of mind at least, if they're suffering or someone around them is suffering and is passing.

RAY: Well, you know what the difference is? That's a great point you brought up. You're talking about someone who's going to jump out of a plane wearing a parachute, and someone who's going to jump out of a plane at ten thousand feet not wearing a parachute.

GABBY: Which one am I?

RAY: You're the one not wearing a parachute at the moment.

GABBY: [Laughs] Yes.

RAY: And the thought is really terrifying! As a Christian, when I pass through death, my fear will be in direct relation to my faith. It's like, if I'm gonna jump out of a plane, my faith in the parachute will dissipate my fears. If I trust that parachute a hundred percent, I'm not going to be fearful at all. I'm going say, "Let's go! Let's do it! Let's jump! It's going to be fifteen miles an hour, and I'll land on my feet."

GABBY: Mm-hmm.

RAY: But if I don't have faith, it's gonna be terrifying. So I don't want you to be on your deathbed terrified, Gabby.

GABBY: Ha!

RAY: I want you to have faith in Jesus and say, "I know my Redeemer lives. I know I'm passed from death to life because I'm trusting in this God-given Savior." So please think about what we talked about, with a sense of sobriety. Those people that are Christians have been praying for you, and you're listening today because of their prayers. And if it's okay with you, I'd like to give you a little book that we've published called *The Bible's Four Gospels*. May I give it to you?

GABBY: Sure! Yes, I'll read it.

RAY: Well, thank you so much. I appreciate your honesty. Would you be embarrassed if I pray with you?

GABBY: No. Okay.

RAY: Father, I pray for Gabby. Thank you that she listened today. I pray today she'll think soberly about her secret sins and what you did on the cross for her and find a place of true repentance because of your mercy. In Jesus' name we pray. Amen.

Chapter 6

OBEDIENCE PROTECTS

The thief on the cross had a big problem: he was nailed to a cross. So he turned to Jesus. But it wasn't to have his big problem fixed; it was to have his sins forgiven. He was a thief, and because he was aware of his sin, the fear of the Lord filled his dying soul. But there was another thief who had the same big problem. He, too, was nailed to a cross, but he wanted a solution for his physical problem, not his spiritual problem.

> Then one of the criminals who were hanged blasphemed Him, saying, "If You are the Christ, save Yourself and us."
> But the other, answering, rebuked him, saying, "Do you not even fear God, seeing you are under the same condemnation?" (Luke 23:39–40)

The thief on the cross who feared the Lord came to faith in Jesus. It seems the Roman guards didn't get the memo that says when people become Christians, their problems are fixed and they begin a wonderful new life in Christ, right? The guards took a spear and broke both legs of the thief, adding to his agony. Then he suffocated to death from the fluids in his lungs.

To tell sinners that Jesus fixes all our problems and gives us a wonderful new life is both disingenuous and unbiblical. Only if we want to harden the world to the true gospel should we go ahead and tell people that Jesus will fix all their problems. But then we should also give them a Bible that removes John the Baptist being beheaded (Matthew 14:1–12), Stephen being stoned to death (Acts 7:54–60), and King Herod putting James to death by the sword (Acts 12:2). Then, we should cross out the verses that speak of fiery trials, much tribulation, the inevitability of persecution, and the real probability that they will be hated for the name of Jesus.

And when our hearers decide it's time for Jesus to fix their problems, they will ask him into their hearts rather than repent of their sin. That will certainly produce a false conversion, adding to the millions who have already fallen away and become angry that Jesus didn't do what we said he would and solve their problems whenever they pray. In this misrepresentation of the gospel, sin is glossed over, and the prospect of future punishment isn't even mentioned. We need to share the full reality of the Scriptures—God's judgment and mercy—for humans to truly turn from their sin and live obedient lives.

"GOOD" PEOPLE STILL SIN

A certain man is a law-abiding citizen. One day he falls into temptation and steals $20,000 from his workplace to pay a gambling debt. Nobody knows he took the money because he carefully rigged the books. But in time he feels extremely guilty—so guilty he decides to pay the money back. Does that even the scales? Is justice satisfied? Of course not. If he is found out, he might still go to jail for theft. Consider what Scripture says about a similar scenario: "People do not despise a thief if he steals to satisfy himself when he is starving. Yet when he is found, he must restore sevenfold; he may have to give up all the substance of his house" (Proverbs 6:30–31).

Serious transgressions of the law always call for retribution. Sin is an electromagnet for punishment. Scripture warns that *every* transgression will receive a just reward:

> Therefore we must give the more earnest heed to the things we have heard, lest we drift away. For if the word spoken through angels proved stead-fast, and every transgression and disobedience

received a just reward, how shall we escape if we neglect so great a salvation? (Hebrews 2:1–3)

The major reason evil people don't give earnest heed to the gospel is that they don't believe they are evil. They don't believe there is anything to fear. Criminals who believe that they are law-abiding citizens have no reason to fear the police. And sinners' willful ignorance of God's standards makes them complacent about their own salvation. They expect God to bend to their every whim while believing all is well.

Paul addressed this ignorance in Athens:

Truly, these times of ignorance God overlooked, but now commands all men everywhere to repent, because He has appointed a day on which He will judge the world in righteousness by the Man whom He has ordained. He has given assurance of this to all by raising Him from the dead. (Acts 17:30–31)

The natural inclination is for people to believe that all God requires is that they live a good life. And if by chance people slip morally, their good will outweigh the bad. They think morality is like the withdrawals and deposits in a bank account. If the balance becomes overdrawn, the deposit of some good deeds will lift it up again, and the manager will be happy. There is a way that seems right to people, and they think it's the key that will open heaven's door.

Still, there are many people nowadays who start to protest the moment that we mention to sinners the necessity of repentance or obedience. They maintain that all one needs to do to be saved is "believe" in Jesus. But they make two big errors. The first is this: we are not saved by believing in Jesus. We are saved by the grace of God alone (see Ephesians 2:8–9). We believe in Jesus to receive the grace that saves. Faith is just the vehicle that delivers that precious grace. To receive grace, we obey the command to repent and believe, and the fruit of our repentance will be an obedient heart—one that delights to do God's will. Again, grace alone saves us. But the way to obtain grace is to do what Jesus commanded—to repent and believe (see Mark 1:15).

Those who say obedience is not evidence of salvation for the Christian skate heavily on thin ice. The apostle Paul wrote to the believers at Thessalonica, reminding them of the day "when the Lord Jesus is revealed from heaven with His mighty angels, in flaming fire taking vengeance on those who do not know God, *and on those who do not obey the gospel of our Lord Jesus Christ*" (2 Thessalonians 1:7–8, emphasis added).

Without true repentance and obedience, we have people who think they are "good" even though they are still tied to their sinful human behavior. In an article entitled "Why Ethical People Make Unethical Choices," author Ron Carucci says the following:

> Despite good intentions, organizations set themselves up for ethical catastrophes by creating environments in which people feel forced to make choices they could never have imagined. Former Federal Prosecutor Serina Vash says, "When I first began prosecuting corruption, I expected to walk into rooms and find the vilest people. I was shocked to find ordinarily good people I could well have had coffee with that morning. And they were *still good people* who'd made terrible choices."[29]

Deny the reality of sin, and you will daily be shocked by human behavior. The nicest of people who don't fear God will lie to you and steal from you. This is because the sweetest of us has a heart that is both deceitful and desperately wicked: "The heart is deceitful above all things, and desperately wicked; who can know it?" (Jeremiah 17:9).

Deny your sinful nature, and you set yourself up to fall. Acknowledge it, and you identify your most formidable enemy. The hidden enemy that we often don't detect is ourselves. Give place to the devil, and he will devour you as a roaring lion (see 1 Peter 5:8).

INATTENTIONAL BLINDNESS AND OUR CONSCIENCE

Music takes us into another world. It can lift us from the boredom of everyday life and transport us to a land of great joy. The experience can be intensified with earbuds or high-quality, custom-fitted headphones that cancel external noise. However, as with so many great things, there's a side effect. When I try to get the attention of any of these music lovers to ask them to join me on camera, they are often so caught up in their music, it's as though I don't exist. I watch them walk by, then cross the street, ride on bikes, and drive cars, all in a blinding world of sound.

This is a documented phenomenon. Dr. Richard Lichenstein with his colleagues from the University of Maryland School of Medicine and the University of Maryland Medical Center in Baltimore studied reports of train and motor vehicle crashes involving pedestrians wearing headphones and published the findings in *Injury Prevention*.

Researchers reviewed 116 accident cases from 2004 to 2011 in which injured pedestrians were documented to be using headphones. Seventy percent of the 116 accidents resulted in death to the pedestrian…The increased incidence of accidents over the years closely corresponds to

documented rising popularity of auditory tech-
nologies with headphones.[30]

The team even coined the phrase "inattentional
blindness" to describe the distraction caused by elec-
tronical devices.

Sadly, stories like this one are not uncommon.
One recent study found that the number of pedestrians who have been killed or injured while wearing
headphones had more than tripled in six years.[31]

The five senses of hearing, sight, touch, taste,
and smell weren't given to us solely for pleasure. Even
though we can enjoy good music, stand in awe of a
beautiful sunset, tenderly touch a loved one in our
arms, breathe in a mouthwatering fragrance, and
indulge in delicious food, our senses also play a vital
role in self-preservation. We back away from a vicious
dog, avoid touching a prickly cactus, spit out bitter
food, retreat when we smell a skunk—and become
alarmed to danger when a train blasts a warning horn.

The fear of God should sound an alarm in our
conscience when danger is near. That's why the Bible
calls it "the beginning of wisdom" (Proverbs 9:10).
Those who cancel its sound are unwise.

Of course, there are subtle ways in which sound
is canceled. A natural buildup of ear wax can slowly
dull a person's hearing by blocking the ear canal. The

wax prevents sound waves from entering the inner ear, resulting in conductive hearing loss. And like gradual deafness, a dulled conscience doesn't usually happen overnight. It can come to us slowly and subtly in the form of small moral compromises. It may come as sharing or listening to a little bit of gossip, hearing blasphemy and not feeling shocked, listening to music that contains a sinful message, or even smiling at a not-so-clean joke. A person's conscience may become seared because of a glance at a pleasurable but sinful sight that doesn't alarm us as it should. Jesus said that if your eye causes you to sin, "pluck it out and cast it from you. It is better for you to enter into life with one eye, rather than having two eyes, to be cast into hell fire" (Matthew 18:9).

Sin leads us onto a railway line and blinds us to the danger. We must *always* be alarmed by it. The book Proverbs tells us, "Do not enter the path of the wicked, and do not walk in the way of evil. Avoid it, do not travel on it; turn away from it and pass on" (Proverbs 4:14–16). Sin is a drop of deadly poison in a glass of pure water. While the world laughs at the thought and drinks iniquity like water, we know better. To be alarmed means to have "an anxious awareness of danger."[32] That's our attitude to lust, lying, theft, blasphemy, anger, bitterness, hatred, forni- cation, adultery, and every other tiny seed of sin the enemy tries to plant in our hearts. And the God-given means of halting all evil and preserving our souls is the fear of the Lord.

The Bible gives us insight into how the deadly poison drops into the water and how it then works: "Beware, brethren, lest there be in any of you an evil heart of unbelief in departing from the living God; but exhort one another daily, while it is called 'Today,' lest any of you be hardened through the deceitfulness of sin" (Hebrews 3:12–13). With this in mind, let's slip into the mind of David to see how our consciences can be blinded through the deceitfulness of sin.

The Scriptures tell us King David saw a woman bathing, desired her, and had her brought to him. She was married, but that didn't stop him from committing adultery. A short time later, he found out she was pregnant with his child. He tried to cover his tracks, but that didn't work. So, he had her husband killed, and then he took Bathsheba as his wife. David went from the pleasure of adultery to the pain of murder.

This incident should make us tremble. It reminds us of the deceitfulness of sin and how each of us needs to have a conscience that is void of offense toward God and others (see Acts 24:16). This is because conscience is a small voice and sin is a giant. When unbelief comes onto the scene, the giant of sin can easily overshadow us as it did with David.

We can learn a lot about our conscience and temptation from the Venus flytrap. It has a reddish interior and emits a fragrance that fools insects into thinking it's an attractive flower. Inside, there are tiny, sensitive hairs that only respond if touched twice within a span of twenty seconds. This means it doesn't snap shut on raindrops or other false alarms. The first time a hair is touched, it sends an electrical signal along the surface of the trap. With the second touch, the trap slams shut on its victim. The plant then becomes a stomach, sealing the trap so that no air gets in or out. That kills the insect. Lunch is then served.

When David was first tempted to look toward the fragrant flower as she bathed herself, he had time to turn away. Temptation is not sin. Jesus was tempted, as we are, and yet was without sin (Hebrews 4:15). David had time to hear his conscience and get out of the trap, but he didn't. He stayed, and sin pulled him further into its grip. But when it led him to murder, he had somebody else do it for him. He put his crime at arm's length.

Every day, millions, like David, give themselves to sexual sin. For many, the result is an unwanted pregnancy, and, like David, they have attempted to put their problem at arm's length by paying an abortionist to take the life of the child.

Sin in our hearts will eventually poison us against Jesus. He will offend us with his words—because they expose and condemn the sin we try to hide. And it all begins with a heart of unbelief that is deceived into thinking that no one will know if we sin…just a little. And so, the conscience is seared into inaction.

Paul spoke of his absolute priority when it came to dealing with his own conscience: "This being so, I myself always *strive* to have a conscience without offense toward God and men" (Acts 24:16, emphasis added). Allow me to go synonym-crazy for a moment as we consider the word *strive*. Paul endeavored, aimed, aspired, made every effort, exerted himself, did his best, did his utmost, labored, worked, toiled, strained, struggled, fought, contended, and warred to make sure he had a conscience that was without offense. But he didn't leave it there. His was a conscience without offense primarily toward God and then toward man. It was his fear of God giving him reason to engage in the battle against sin.

Dr. Martyn Lloyd-Jones once preached,

Is the fear of the Lord the dominating principle of your life? Are you constantly living your life as under God and under his all-seeing eye? Are you living to the glory of God and to his praise? That is what you were made for. That is what you're meant to do. That is what the fear of the Lord really means…Is your life a God-dominated life? It was said of somebody that he was a God-intoxicated man. We should all be like that. The thing that should govern our every action, our every thought, is the fear of the Lord—the realization that the great God who made the whole cosmos is still there. And that we are responsible to him.[33]

God has given every human being a conscience to help keep us from sin. Once we lose the fear of the Lord, we begin to give in to temptation—little by little—until our consciences are blinded and we no longer seek God. To keep our consciences from becoming blinded to the reality of our sin, we should always be asking ourselves, *Does God dominate my life?*

THE FEAR OF THE LORD IS OUR IRON DOME

Most people misunderstand what it means to live in the fear of the Lord. It doesn't mean that we live in terror of God, worried that any moment he will lose patience and kill us because we have a sinful thought or yielded to a temptation to overindulge in ice cream. To walk in the fear of the Lord means the exact opposite. It means we can have a confident assurance that the enemy cannot devour us.

Take Ashkelon, for example. It is a city on the coast of Israel, not too far from Tel Aviv—just north of the troubled Gaza Strip. On a recent Sunday, as civil defense sirens filled the air across the city, people ran from their cars to seek shelter.

Hiding under a tree, a man tried to comfort his teenage daughter.

"Don't worry," he said, "it will be fine, the Iron Dome will save us."

As he spoke, the Iron Dome's air-defense interceptor missiles streaked into the intense blue sky, making six rockets fired at Ashkelon by the Palestinian Islamist movement Hamas explode into faraway white puffs. As in the majority of cases since Hamas started raining rockets on Israel on Monday—a total of 2,800 by now—there were no casualties or major damage.[34]

The defense system began operating in 2011 and was built and maintained by funding from the United States, costing a massive $1.6 billion. However, judging by the number of lives saved, it has been worth every penny. The Iron Dome is made up of a network of batteries and radar and is programmed to fire at incoming rockets heading for populated areas. It ignores those that are likely to fall in the desert.

The fear of the Lord is the secret place of the Most High. It puts us in the shadow of the Almighty. It is an impenetrable iron dome that shoots down incoming rockets from the enemy. We submit to God and resist the devil, knowing that he will flee (see James 4:7). If I live in obedience to God's law, the devil can't get a foothold on my life because I serve God, not sin. Joseph was a man who feared the Lord. When Potiphar's wife tempted him to sin, this godly fear pressed him to do the right thing.

> So it was, as she spoke to Joseph day by day, that he did not heed her, to lie with her or to be with her.
>
> But it happened about this time, when Joseph went into the house to do his work, and none of the men of the house was inside, that she caught him by his garment, saying, "Lie with me." But he left his garment in her hand, and fled and ran outside. (Genesis 39:10–12)

Joseph ran, and David fell (see 2 Samuel 11). The difference was that Joseph saw the danger signs, believed them, and in doing so, protected himself through his fear of the Lord. It chained the beast. When we fear God, we see sin as an ocean where we once swam. In it, we lived, moved, and had our being. But Jesus rescued us before we were pulled under by its current. Now, the fear of the Lord keeps us out. Had David feared God when his eyes began to boggle at the bathing Bathsheba, he would never have committed adultery and committed murder. How blessed we are to have the Scriptures teach us about the self-preserving nature of the fear of God.

How could I ever follow David in committing adultery when I know God is keeping watch on the evil and the good? It means that I say with Joseph, when he was tempted by Potiphar's lusty wife, "How then can I do this great wickedness, and sin against God?" (Genesis 39:9). It offers us a quiet assurance of safety in this life and into the next. The fear of the Lord is my protector. And that is very precious. With it, I'm a Joseph. Without it, I'm a David…and even a Judas.

WITNESSING ENCOUNTER

The following transcript was taken from a video entitled "He Didn't Fear God, but Watch Him Change." In this conversation, a young man begins to understand what it really means to fear the Lord.

> RAY: What's the most important thing in life to you? Is it, uh, the pursuit of happiness? Happiness is your most important pursuit. Is that correct?
>
> ISAAC: Pretty much, in a sense, yes, yes.

RAY: Okay, I'm going to give you a scenario. You find a package on the side of the road. Looks kind of important. You open it up. It's got a name and address on it. You open it up, and inside, you find some jewelry. It's a necklace. So you think, *Oh, this is kind of strange.* So you take it to get it valued and find that it's worth over a million dollars. And the guy says he'll give you cash for it—over a million dollars. Would you keep it?

ISAAC: If it had the name on it, you know what I mean—it wasn't sent to me—then obviously, yes. Like, I'd have to return it. You know what I mean?

RAY: So, there's something more important to you than happiness. It's righteousness. You want to do that which is right rather than that [which] would make—because that jewelry would give you money to make you happy. You'd get a Lamborghini with that sort of money. You could set up a business. You'd have lots of things in life that would make you happy. But it's more important for you to do that which is right. Not just because of the fear of punishment but because it's the right thing.

ISAAC: Yes, honestly. You got it pretty down. Um, yes. For me, yes, I want happiness too. You know what I mean? But before happiness, you know righteousness is, you know, one thing that I'd rather do first. You know what I mean?

RAY: Why?

ISAAC: Because it's, man, like if—man, my conscience—if I do something bad or messed up, you know what I mean, I don't feel good. You know what I mean? I gotta fix it. You know what I'm saying?

RAY: So, you're saying you'd do it for conscience's sake? What about the fear of God? Do you fear God?

ISAAC: No, dude. No. If I'm going to fix something, it's for myself, not because of fear. You know what I mean? Like, I know, I know there's people, that would be, like, "Well, I gotta fix, you know, my sins or something, because I don't wanna go to hell." You know what I mean? Like [expletive] that, dude, like—

RAY: So you don't fear God?

ISAAC: No, dude, I do that for myself. You know what I mean? And not—if there is a God, I don't think you should fear him. You know what I mean?

RAY: You know, the Bible says the fear of God is the beginning of wisdom. What do you fear in life?

ISAAC: [Expletive], dude. I fear in life, um, losing my family. You know what I mean?

RAY: Death?

ISAAC: Uh, death? I've never really faced death. You know what I mean? But, um—

RAY: Well, that's a legitimate fear, to fear death. You don't want to die. Do you know what death is, according to the Bible? Do you know?

ISAAC: No, I don't. What is it?

RAY: Wages!

ISAAC: Wages?

RAY: Yes, the Bible says, "The wages of sin is death" [Romans 6:23]. God says he's paying you in death for your sins. He's given you the death sentence because he says sin is so evil. It's like a judge gives a criminal who's murdered three young girls the death sentence. He says, "This is what you've earned. This is your wages. This is what's due to you." Do you think you're that evil that God should put you to death, that he should give you capital punishment?

ISAAC: No, I don't think he—no! No!

RAY: You know why you think that? Well, because your image of God is incorrect. You don't fear God. You don't see him for what he is. So let me just ask you a couple of questions to see if I can put the fear of God in you, because it's the beginning of wisdom. The minute you fear God, you're beginning to get wise. You think you're a good person?

ISAAC: Uh, no.

RAY: So you're doing things you know are morally wrong?

ISAAC: Okay, I'm not a good person, but I'm not a bad person either. You know what I mean? Like—

RAY: Okay, let's see. How many lies have you told in your life?

ISAAC: [Expletive], man. A lot.

RAY: Have you stolen something?

ISAAC: Uh.

RAY: So you're a lying thief?

ISAAC: Pretty much. You know what I mean?

RAY: Have you ever used God's name in vain?

ISAAC: Like—like when someone says, like, [expletive]? Like, uh, yes.

RAY: Would you use your mother's name as a cuss word?

ISAAC: Nah.

RAY: Why not?

ISAAC: I don't know, dude. It doesn't make sense. Like—

RAY: Because it would be a horrible thing to do! Instead of using a filth word beginning with *s* to express disgust—to put her name in its place?

ISAAC: That's true.

RAY: But that's what you've done with the name of God, which is holy. You know, godly Jews won't even speak God's name or even write it down, but you've taken his holy name and used it in place of that filth word to express disgust. And that's called blasphemy.

ISAAC: Yes.

RAY: So serious, Isaac, it's punishable by death in the Old Testament.

ISAAC: Mm-hmm.

RAY: Do you still think you're a good person?

ISAAC: [Expletive], man. Well, according to the Bible, no, I'm not. You know what I mean?

RAY: You know, Jesus said, "If you look at a woman and lust for her, you commit adultery with her in your heart" [Matthew 5:28, author's paraphrase]. Have you ever looked at a woman with lust?

ISAAC: Yes.

RAY: Have you had sex before marriage?

ISAAC: Yes.

RAY: So, Isaac, I'm not judging you; this is for you to judge yourself. You've told me you're a lying, thieving, fornicating, blasphemous, adulterer at heart. And you have to face God on judgment day, whom you don't fear. If he judges you by the Ten Commandments, you going to be innocent or guilty?

ISAAC: Guilty. Like, hardcore.

RAY: So you've earned your wages.

ISAAC: [Expletive] yes, dude, but I don't wanna die yet, man.

RAY: Well, you know what Jesus said? He said, "Fear not him who has power to kill your body and afterwards do no more, but fear him who has power to kill your body and cast your soul into hell. Fear him" [Luke 12:4–5, author's paraphrase]. Imagine standing before God, and all those secret sins came out—all that looking at pornography and doing things you knew were wrong and those inappropriate sexual thoughts—they all come out as evidence of your guilt. Jesus said, "Every idle word a man speaks, he'll give an account thereof on the day of judgment" [Matthew 12:36, author's paraphrase]. So, if you're guilty on judgment day, will you go to heaven or hell?

ISAAC: Dude, I'm guilty, man. I don't think I could come back from it. You know what I mean?

RAY: You'd go to hell?

ISAAC: Pretty much, yes.

RAY: And you can't come back from it. Do you know what you'd do if you're in court and you can't justify yourself? Do you know what you'd do?

ISAAC: Yes, I'd go to prison.

RAY: No, you throw yourself on the mercy of the judge.

ISAAC: Oh, yes.

RAY: You say, "Judge, I'm so sorry. Please show me mercy." And the Bible says God is rich in mercy to all that call upon him [Psalm 86:5]. He has no pleasure in the death of the wicked [Ezekiel 33:11]. He doesn't want to give you justice. He doesn't want you to go to the lake of fire. He wants you to be saved. Now, how can God show you mercy? Do you know?

ISAAC: I don't really know.

RAY: Well, Jesus suffered and died on the cross. Didn't you know that?

ISAAC: Yes, I know that.

RAY: Well, most people know that, but they don't know this—so Isaac, listen up real close, because this is life-changing. You and I broke God's law, the Ten Commandments; Jesus paid the fine. That's what happened on that cross. That's why he said, "It is finished!" [John 19:30] just before he died. Isaac, if you're in court and someone pays your fine, a judge can legally let you go. He can say, "Isaac, there's a stack of speeding fines here. This is deadly serious. Ten thousand people a year die because of speeding in the US, but someone's paid the fine, so you're out of here. You're free to go." Even though you're guilty, you walk because someone paid your fine. And even though you and I are guilty before God, worthy of the death sentence, worthy of damnation, God can let us go. He can take the death sentence off us and let us live because Jesus paid the fine in full. That means God can do that which is legal and right and just and still extend mercy toward us. Is this making sense?

ISAAC: Yes.

RAY: Isaac, you know how you love to sin, how you love looking at pornography and fornicating? God will so change your heart that you will love righteousness. That's what happens when you're born again, when you ask God to forgive you.

ISAAC: Uh-huh.

RAY: The Bible says, "Riches profit not on the day of wrath, but righteousness delivers from death" [Proverbs 11:4, author's paraphrase]. So think of the day of judgment and think how Christ died for your sins and think of how God commands you to repent and trust in the Savior. God commands all men everywhere to repent because he has appointed a day in which he'll judge the world in righteousness.

ISAAC: Yes.

RAY: If you'll turn from sin and say, "God forgive me. Change my heart. I put my trust in Jesus," God will make you righteous in his sight. He'll forgive all your sins in an instant. He'll wash you clean. He'll put a robe of righteousness on you so that you live. Isaac, you've been so gracious and so patient with me in listening. You going to think about what we talked about?

ISAAC: Yes, for sure, dude. Like, it's something I gotta think about. You know what I mean?

RAY: Because you don't know when you're going die. You could leave here, and death could seize upon you, so there's a sense of urgency. Do you have a Bible at home?

ISAAC: I think so. I think my mom has one. Yes.

RAY: Is your mom a Christian?

ISAAC: Catholic.

RAY: So, Isaac, if you were to die today and God gave you justice, you'd be damned. You'd go to hell. There are two things you must do to be saved: you must repent and trust in Jesus. When are you going to do that?

ISAAC: How do I do that?

RAY: Well, if you ever had an argument with a girlfriend, and there's, like, a barrier between you, and you just can't talk to each other, and both of you are like a couple of dogs with the fur up on the back of your neck—you're angry and prideful—and you turn to her and say, "Honey, I'm so sorry," and she says, "So am I," and you cry, and you reconcile. Just go to God and say, "God, I'm so sorry. I've been a rebel. I've loved that which is wrong. Please forgive me." That's called contrition, or being sorry for your sins, and the Bible says, "Godly sorrow works repentance" [2 Corinthians 7:10, author's paraphrase]. So if you'll just get before the Lord and confess and forsake your sins, and say, "God, please forgive me. I'm a sinner," and trust in Jesus, God will hear your prayer. The Bible says that. He says, "I'll not despise a contrite or a sorrowful heart" [Psalm 51:17, author's paraphrase].

ISAAC: So, like a prayer?

RAY: Yes. Do you mind if I pray with you?

ISAAC: Right now? Uh, yes. Sure, like, I don't even really know how to do it though, so—

RAY: Well, let me pray. Father, I pray for Isaac, that you'll give him understanding, that this day he'll yield his life to you in genuine repentance, that he'll understand the issues of life and death and what Jesus did on the cross. Today may he call upon you and trust in your mercy, and pass from death to life. In Jesus' name we pray. Amen.

ISAAC: Amen.

RAY: Isaac, I'm going give you a little booklet called *The Bible's Four Gospels* and another one called *Save Yourself Some Pain*.[35] Okay? Hey, thank you for listening to me. I really appreciate it.

ISAAC: No problem, man. Yes, you know, this was a good talk. You know what I mean? Like, it's always good to have, you know, these types of talks. You know what I mean?

Chapter 7

JUDAS IS THE WARNING

Many Christians have wondered how a disciple of Jesus could betray him. Didn't Judas pray with the other disciples, "Do not lead us into temptation, but deliver us from the evil one" (Matthew 6:13)? Why didn't God answer the prayer of one of Jesus' closest followers?

The Bible says that we are all drawn away by our lusts: "Every man is tempted, when he is drawn away of his own lust, and enticed" (James 1:14 KJV). When we are drawn away, we go somewhere. With lust, we are drawn away from the light and into the darkness. We are taken from God toward the devil. And nothing succeeds in doing that like the twin evils: the love of money and the love of sexual sin. Those who give themselves to such sins show there is no fear of God before their eyes: "Indeed, you are doing away with fear, and you are diminishing meditation before God" (Job 15:4 AMP).

THE TEMPTATION OF MONEY

To see what it was that led Judas onto the path of betrayal, let's peep through the keyhole of Scripture.

> Then Mary took a pound of very expensive perfume of pure nard, and she poured it on Jesus' feet and wiped His feet with her hair; and the house was filled with the fragrance of the perfume. But Judas Iscariot, one of His disciples, the one who was going to betray Him, said, "Why was this perfume not sold for three hundred denarii and [the money] given to the poor?" Now he said this, not because he cared about the poor [for he had never cared about them], but because he was a thief; and since he had the money box [serving as treasurer for the twelve disciples], he used to pilfer what was put into it. (John 12:3–6 AMP)

Judas was trusted to look after the finances. There's a test for any human being—to be left alone with money. And no doubt there was no shortage. Jesus was wildly popular, and a lot of support came in to keep the ministry rolling (see Luke 8:1–3).

Many contributed to support Jesus and his followers. If someone wanted to give toward the ministry, it was likely this person would be discreet, slipping a little something into the hand of one of

Jesus' disciples, because Jesus often spoke about how we should give without blowing a trumpet for the world to see. The gift would then be given to the trustworthy treasurer. Perhaps some benefactors went directly to Judas and handed him the money, and he had the thought that no one would know if he kept it. An evil heart of unbelief accommodates sin. Of course, *someone* would know.

We don't know when Judas began stealing money from the collection bag. However, I can't help but wonder if he was listening when Jesus said these words of warning about covetousness and the heart:

> Do not lay up for yourselves treasures on earth, where moth and rust destroy and where thieves break in and steal; but lay up for yourselves treasures in heaven, where neither moth nor rust destroys and where thieves do not break in and steal. For where your treasure is, there your heart will be also. (Matthew 6:19–21)

Despite all Jesus' teachings and miracles, Judas found that he could not serve God and mammon. He ended up loving one and hating the other (see v. 24). In his pursuit of worldly blessings, he was blinded to the spiritual blessings Jesus was offering. Such is the nature of a covetous heart. "The love of money is a root of all kinds of evil" (1 Timothy 6:10). The root of greed grew silently in Judas' heart, hidden from human eyes.

THE DENIAL OF JESUS' DEITY

Judas Iscariot lacked the fear of God. This can be seen in his betrayal, but it is also revealed in his interactions with Jesus:

> When evening had come, He sat down with the twelve. Now as they were eating, He said, "Assuredly, I say to you, one of you will betray Me."
>
> And they were exceedingly sorrowful, and each of them began to say to Him, "Lord, is it I?"
>
> He answered and said, "He who dipped his hand with Me in the dish will betray Me. The Son of Man indeed goes just as it is written of Him, but woe to that man by whom the Son of Man is betrayed! It would have been good for that man if he had not been born."
>
> Then Judas, who was betraying Him, answered and said, "Rabbi, is it I?"
>
> He said to him, "You have said it." (Matthew 26:20–25)

When the disciples said, "Lord, is it I?" the Greek word translated "Lord" is *kurios*. This is the same word used in Matthew 11:25: "At that time Jesus answered and said, 'I thank You, Father, Lord of heaven and earth, that You have hidden these things from the wise and prudent and have revealed them to babes.'" *Kurios* can be used to refer to an earthly master, but clearly Jesus wasn't doing that when he praying to his Father. In addition, *kurios* was the word used in place of the divine name—YHWH—when the Hebrew Old Testament was translated into Greek.[36] Therefore, when it's used in the New Testament, it carries a lot of weight.

Of course, there was one disciple who didn't address Jesus as "Lord." Judas called him "Rabbi," which merely means "my distinguished teacher."[37] And this wasn't the only time. The same telltale word passes through his deceitful lips a little later in Matthew's gospel:

> While He was still speaking, behold, Judas, one of the twelve, with a great multitude with swords and clubs, came from the chief priests and elders of the people. Now His betrayer had given them a sign, saying, "Whomever I kiss, He is the One; seize Him." Immediately he went up to Jesus and said, "Greetings, Rabbi!" and kissed Him. (26:47–49)

Despite seeing Jesus' miracles, experiencing his loving-kindness, and hearing his unprecedented words, Judas confined Jesus to being a mere teacher. He denied his deity.

But if we understand the nature and character of our God—that he is not only loving and kind but also the sovereign Lord who delights in judgment and righteousness—we have good reason to rejoice:

> Thus says the LORD:
>> "Let not the wise man glory in his wisdom,
>> let not the mighty man glory in his might,
>> nor let the rich man glory in his riches;
>> but let him who glories glory in this,
>> that he understands and knows Me,
>> that I am the LORD, exercising lovingkindness, judgment, and righteousness in the earth.
>> For in these I delight," says the LORD.
> (Jeremiah 9:23–24)

Contrary to Judas' small view of Jesus, Scripture describes him as "He who is the blessed and only Potentate, the King of kings and Lord of lords, who alone has immortality, dwelling in unapproachable light, whom no man has seen or can see, to whom be honor and everlasting power" (1 Timothy 6:15–16). Even more pointed is the New Testament's description of Jesus' glorious return, "when the Lord Jesus is revealed from heaven with His mighty angels, in flaming fire taking vengeance on those who do not know God, and on those who do not obey the gospel of our Lord Jesus Christ" (2 Thessalonians 1:7–8).

Having a right understanding of God puts us in our rightful place. We are the lowly creature; he is the Creator. We are temporary; he is eternal. And he holds our life's breath in his hands. Perhaps the greatest lesson we can learn in life is that we cannot achieve anything without him: "I am the vine, you are the branches. He who abides in Me, and I in him, bears much fruit; for *without Me you can do nothing*" (John 15:5, emphasis added).

Without God, we can do nothing. All of our achievements—no matter how significant they may seem—won't amount to a hill of beans in the light of eternity. Everything is chasing the wind. It is futile. There is only one everlasting kingdom. Everything else will turn to dust, whether it be human or beast, fish or reptile, mountain or a man-made monument. Moth and rust will corrupt it in time, and it will amount to nothing.

Yet Judas didn't see Jesus as the Lord of lords or as someone to be feared. He saw Jesus as merely a rabbi, like so many others saw Jesus during that time. This incorrect view of Jesus' deity and a lack of fear of the Lord led Judas to his ultimate fate.

THE SEARED CONSCIENCE

How could it be that Judas went from being a thief to being the facilitator of the crucifixion of the Son of God? Jesus called Judas his friend (Matthew 26:50), and yet what Judas did was utterly hateful. The answer is that when people love darkness, they naturally hate the light. Jesus warned that he would be hated because he accused the world of sin: "The world cannot hate you, but it hates Me because I testify of it that its works are evil" (John 7:7).

It's evident by his theft that Judas had a seared conscience. It allowed him to steal. And when a conscience allows theft, it will also allow other sins because its alarm has been silenced. Perhaps other sinful thoughts crept into the heart of Judas as attractive women approached him and trusted him with their financial support. We don't know his experience, but we do know where sin begins: "For as he thinks in his heart, so is he" (Proverbs 23:7).

The betrayal of Jesus started in the soil of Judas' heart, and it grew because Judas didn't fear God. The secret resentment that Judas had for Jesus eventually manifested when he realized he could kill two birds with one stone. He could hand Jesus over to his enemies and make some cash at the same time. The money he was stealing from the bag wasn't enough. Sin is never satisfied.

Let's look again at Hebrews 3:13 in the *Amplified Bible* to see what sin did to him:

> But continually encourage one another every day, as long as it is called "Today" [and there is an opportunity], so that none of you will be hardened [into settled rebellion] by the deceitfulness of sin [its cleverness, delusive glamour, and sophistication].

There are many who once raised their hands in worship of the Savior but who now shake their fists at him. They have become enemies of the cross of Jesus Christ:

> Brethren, join in following my example, and note those who so walk, as you have us for a pattern. For many walk, of whom I have told you often, and now tell you even weeping, that they are the enemies of the cross of Christ: whose end is destruction, whose god is their belly, and whose glory is in their shame—who set their mind on earthly things. (Philippians 3:17–19)

Judas didn't expect the wages of his sin to be death. He didn't expect his end to be destruction. He didn't even keep his thirty bloodstained pieces of silver. His money amounted to nothing—just like everything this world treasures. One can't help but wonder if he was paying attention when Jesus said, "Do not lay up for yourselves treasures on earth, where moth and rust destroy and where thieves break in and steal; but lay up for yourselves treasures in heaven, where neither moth nor rust destroys and where thieves do not break in and steal" (Matthew 6:19–20).

THE JUDAS IN US

Sadly, Judas is typical of many people in this world. Most of us, if left without any fear of God, would betray Jesus for the love of sin. Scriptures describe the wicked as "having eyes full of adultery and that cannot cease from sin, enticing unstable souls. They have a heart trained in covetous practices, and are accursed children" (2 Peter 2:14).

But the fear of the Lord changes the wicked heart. That is why it is essential. Fear leads to humility, and humility draws us to repentance. And it is in true faith and repentance that a person's evil heart is truly changed. George Whitefield said,

> Every man by his own natural will hates God; but when he is turned unto the Lord, by evangelical repentance, then his will is changed; then your consciences, nor hardened and benumbed, shall be quickened and awakened; then your [hard] hearts shall be melted, and your unruly affections shall be crucified. Thus, by that

repentance, the whole soul will be changed, you will have new inclinations, new desires, and new habits.[38]

Scripture tells us, "The secret of the LORD is with those who fear Him" (Psalm 25:14). While the Bible doesn't tell us the exact nature of the secret, I surmise it's a reference to the fact that salvation from death comes to those who fear God and yield to his Lordship. Look at how closely the pathway of mercy follows the fear of the Lord:

> Behold, the eye of the LORD is on those who
> fear Him,
> on those who hope in His mercy,
> to deliver their soul from death,
> and to keep them alive in famine.
> (Psalm 33:18–19)

Jesus has provided a way for our souls to be delivered from death. Think of the abundance of life that exists in those who fear the Lord. As Charles Spurgeon said, "The fear of the Lord, which is the beginning of wisdom, fills the heart, and the goodness of the Lord becomes the source and fountain of that fear in the hearts of all those whom the Lord has blessed with His grace."[39]

And Judas could have had all that. But he didn't because he didn't fear the Lord. And now we face the same choice: follow Judas down the path to destruction or fear the Lord and receive abundant life by his mercy.

WITNESSING ENCOUNTER

The following is from an interesting interview of two young women we titled "Do THIS and You're Messing with Demons."

> RAY: Do you know what an idiom is?
>
> SAM: An idiom?
>
> RAY: I'm going to give you one, and I want you to try and explain it to me. First, I'll ask you if you've ever used it and then explain what it means. If I said to you, "Well, I'll be damned," what does that mean? Have you ever used it?
>
> SAM: Yes, I have.
>
> RAY: Give me a context in which you've used it.
>
> SAM: I've used it in a sense where I've said "Well, I'll be damned if I don't get that trick."
>
> RAY (TO JEN): Have you ever used it?
>
> JEN: Yes, in, like, situations where I'm not expecting an outcome, I'll be like "Well, I'll be damned."
>
> RAY: That's a surprise. I'm surprised. What does it mean to be damned?
>
> JEN: To be, like, cursed?

RAY: Why would you say that as an idiom? I mean, I've tried to research it, and I can't figure it out—why people would say, "Well, I'll be damned."

SAM: It's the same way that people [say], like, "holy…" and then, you know. People don't really take into consideration what they're saying. They just kind of say it, like, "Well, I'll be damned," and then you really take a step back, and realize what you're saying, and you're like, "Wait, I just cursed myself basically."

RAY: Here's another one: "As sure as hell, I'll be there." What does that mean? Would you think hell is sure? Sure as hell? You know, it's a strange thing to say.

SAM: It's a very strange thing. I'm pretty sure hell isn't sure.

RAY: Do you believe in God's existence?

SAM: Not everyone's idea of God, like the biblical, but I do believe in God, in the sense that the universe, the higher power, my spirit guides, my angels.

RAY (TO JEN): And do you believe in God's existence?

JEN: I believe that the universe definitely has a force that works in mysterious ways and definitely comes in like karma and stuff like that. Everything happens for a reason.

RAY: And what you reap, you'll sow; if you do rotten things, rotten things will come back to you.

JEN: Yes.

RAY: Yes, it's just a kind of a law of life.

SAM: Let's say you hex someone or, you know—like jealousy that creates bad energy. Three-fold rule. It usually comes back to you. Like you said, you reap what you sow.

RAY: Are you into spiritism?

SAM: Yes.

RAY: Is that demons?

SAM: No, not whatsoever. That's not in my practice whatsoever.

RAY: Familiar spirits?

SAM: Yes, it's my spirit guides who are usually my ancestors and my angels are, for example, my brother who passed away is one of my angels. My grandma that passed away is one of my angels.

RAY: Do you know what *familiar spirit* means?

SAM: Not necessarily. If you could explain that to me…

RAY: Yes, the Bible says it's actually demons.

SAM: Demons?

RAY: Yes.

SAM: Well, personally I've had experience with both negative and positive energy. Kind of paranormal things, so I can differentiate what is evil and what's not.

RAY: How do you know?

SAM: You can feel it. You can sense it.

RAY: You know how the Bible describes Satan? He's called an angel of light, and yet he's the epitome of evil. Do you know what he does, according to the New Testament? He blinds the minds of people to the gospel. Did you know that?

SAM: No, I didn't.

RAY: Are you familiar with the gospel?

SAM: No.

RAY: Let me share it with you and get your thoughts in a minute. [TO JEN:] Are you familiar with the gospel?

JEN: Neither, no.

RAY (TO SAM): Okay, do you think you're a good person?

SAM: Yes, I know I'm a good person.

RAY (TO JEN): Okay. Do you think you're a good person?

JEN: Yes, I think so. Yes.

RAY: What standard do you judge by? Because everybody thinks they're good. I mean a man who rapes a woman would say, "Oh, I think I'm good, I just felt like it—she deserved it."

SAM: If you move with ill intentions, you know, and everyone knows right from wrong, and I do know that everything that I do is filled with love and positivity.

RAY: Okay, I'm putting that to the test. Can you handle that?

SAM: I think so. [Laughs]

RAY: Can you be honest with me?

SAM: Yes.

RAY: How many lies have you told in your life?

SAM: I can't count how many lies, but I do know that I have lied before in my life.

RAY: What do you call someone who tells lies?

SAM: Dishonest.

RAY: A liar?

SAM: Yes, a liar.

RAY (TO JEN): Have you lied?

JEN: Definitely.

RAY: Have you stolen?

JEN: Definitely.

SAM: Yes, I have.

RAY: Have you ever used God's name in vain?

SAM: Probably.

RAY (TO JEN): What about you?

JEN: Definitely have. Yes.

RAY: Would you use your mother's name as a cuss word?

SAM: No.

RAY: Why not?

SAM: Because it's my mother, and I have the utmost respect for my mother.

RAY: That's right. You'd never do that, and yet you've taken the holy name of God—a name that godly Jews won't even speak, it's so holy— and brought it down to the level of a filth word to express disgust, which is called "blasphemy." So serious, it's punishable by death. Do you still think you're a good person?

SAM: Yes.

RAY: Now, Jesus said if you look with lust, you commit adultery in the heart [Matthew 5:28]. Have you ever looked with lust?

SAM: I think…yes.

RAY (TO JEN): And what about you?

JEN: Yes.

RAY: Have you used God's name in vain?

JEN: Yes.

RAY: Have you had sex before marriage?

JEN: Yes.

SAM: Yes.

RAY: Okay, ladies, I'm not judging you, this is for you, not for me, okay? You've both told me you're lying, thieving, blasphemous, fornicating, adulterers at heart.

JEN: [LAUGHS NERVOUSLY]

SAM: [LAUGHS NERVOUSLY; BLASPHEMES] And when you put it like that, it sounds very negative. But I think that we're all human, and we make mistakes the same way. I don't know. We can re-right our wrongs.

RAY: How do you re-right lust?

SAM: Well, lust is a normal thing, and having sex before marriage, I think, is totally human.

RAY: And so is blasphemy and lying and stealing—it's all human; it comes naturally to us. Now I'm going to ask you another question. On judgment day, if God judges you by the Ten Commandments—we've looked at four of them—would you be innocent or guilty?

SAM: I'm not sure because I don't know all of them. But I think that I'm deemed a good person, and I know I'm very secure within myself and who I am, that no Bible or no person's opinion is going to change how I feel.

RAY: I'm going to give you something that might change how you feel. Jen, if God judges you by the Ten Commandments, would you be innocent or guilty?

JEN: Probably be guilty [of] a few of them. Yes.

RAY: Heaven or hell?

JEN: Hopefully, heaven, but where I go, I go. Where I end up…[SHRUGS]

RAY: You've got God's promise you'll be damned. That's what the Bible says. Now, here's the thing that will change your mind: If you look at the word *good* in the dictionary, there are over forty different definitions. Number one is "moral excellence"—absolute moral perfection. None of us are good in that respect. We're good by human standards; that's the difference. Of course you're a good person by human standards, but not by God's. So, you'd be damned, too, which horrifies me. [TO SAM:] And what does that mean? [POINTS TO SAM'S TATTOO OF THE WORD *MORTEM*]

SAM: This means "death."

RAY: Yes, *mort* means "death." *Mortgage* means "death grip." Did you know that? When someone gets a mortgage for a house, it's a death grip. So *mortem* means "death"?

SAM: Yes, it does.

RAY: Do you know what death is, according to the Bible?

SAM: No, because I'm not a Bible reader, like I said.

RAY: It's "wages." Have you ever heard the Bible verse, "The wages of sin is death" [Romans 6:23]?

SAM: No, I have not.

RAY: Yes, death is [the] payment God gives you for sin. It's like a judge looking at a criminal who has raped three girls and murdered them, and says, "You've earned the death sentence. This is what's due to you. This is your wages." And sin is so serious to God, he's given us capital punishment. So, ladies, I'd be horrified at the thought of both of you being damned— God giving you justice. So, here's a big question: What did God do for guilty sinners so we wouldn't have to go to hell? Do you know?

SAM: I do not know, but, again, I don't believe in that concept of God. I don't believe in the biblical God. Within myself, I know that a god that loves us wouldn't damn us because of human mistakes. And yes, we all make different mistakes. We're all out at a different degree, but my idea of god is not that I'm going to be damned. Just the same way that people tell me I'm going to be damned for my sexual choices.

RAY: Let me come back to you in a minute—don't let me forget, but let me just ask Jen: Would you be concerned if God gave you justice and you ended up damned in hell? Does that concern you? Do you love your life?

JEN: Well, I do love my life, but I wouldn't be too concerned. I don't think there's a heaven and a hell. If I die, my spirit's going somewhere, but I don't think it's these preconceived notions of…

RAY: Horrifies me at the thought of you being damned. [TO SAM:] So, let's get back to what you just said. What you just did, Sam, is violated the first of the Ten Commandments. I did that before I was a Christian. This is where you make up a god to suit yourself. You create a god you feel comfortable with.

SAM: But that's your idea.

RAY: That's right. I did it before I was a Christian. What did God do for guilty sinners so we wouldn't have to be damned—we wouldn't have to go to hell?

SAM: I don't know.

RAY: Let me tell you and get your thoughts on it, okay? And then I'll let you go. I appreciate your patience, Sam. Jesus suffered and died on the cross to take the punishment for the sin of the world. I see you nodding, so you know that. You and I broke God's law, the Ten Commandments. Jesus came and paid the fine. That's what happened on that cross. That's why he said, "It is finished" [John 19:30] just before he died. In other words, the debt has been paid. Sam, if you're in court and someone pays your fine, a judge can legally let you go. He can say, "Sam, there's a stack of speeding fines here. This is deadly serious, but someone's paid them. You're free to go," and he can do that which is legal and right and just. Well, God can legally let you live forever. He can take the death sentence off you because Jesus paid the fine in full so you could go free. Does that make sense?

SAM: It makes complete sense, but it still doesn't pertain to me…

RAY: Yes, and you still listened, and I appreciate that. Then Jesus rose from the dead, defeated our greatest enemy, death itself; and if you'll simply repent of your sins, let them go, turn from them, and trust in Jesus—like you trust a parachute—God promises he'll grant you everlasting life. He'll take death off you because he's rich in mercy.

SAM: I'm sure that's how you feel, but I don't believe in your concept of God and Jesus.

RAY: I know that.

SAM: I'm still going to keep saying that because I'm not going to repent for my sins and the idea that you think.

RAY: You're going to think about what we talked about?

JEN: Probably for five minutes and then go on about my day.

RAY: Okay, please do because my motive is because I care about you. I'm not trying to convert you; I don't want a notch in my belt. I just want you to think about your eternity because this is your precious life we're talking about. And same with you, Sam. Your life is so precious.

SAM: Oh yes, I know.

RAY: I'm just telling you how you can keep it. "He that saves his life will lose it, he that loses his life for my sake," Jesus said, "will keep it"

[Matthew 16:25, author's paraphrase]. And that's what God's offering you—everlasting life as a free gift. I just want you to perhaps give some thought to this, maybe as you lay your head on your pillow tonight and hear your heartbeat in your ear and think of the fragility of life. Just think about what we talked about; that's all I'm asking. Will you do that for me?

SAM: Yes.

Chapter 8

JESUS IS THE WAY

Three men were playing poker in an old hotel. During the game, they heard someone call "Fire!" When two of the men stood to their feet, the third told them to sit down and finish the game because they still had plenty of time. He then said, "I have the key to the exit in my pocket." Again, they heard someone yelling to get out of the building. Both men were beginning to become agitated as they could see flames through a small window above the doorway. The man with the key took it from his pocket, slapped it on the table, and said, "I told you it's okay! Here's the key. Finish the game!" Precious seconds passed as smoke filled the room. When flames suddenly burst through the windows, the men threw down their cards and rushed to the exit. In went the key, but it wouldn't turn—at which the now-shocked man cried, "It's the wrong key!"

Such is the way of the ungodly. Death draws near, the flames of fiery indignation threaten, and

Christians plead. But sinners don't think God will require an account. All is well. These sinners believe they have the issue in hand. "Live a good life," they say. "Believe in God. Do to others as you'd have them do to you. Let your good outweigh your bad. If you're a good person at heart, you'll make it to heaven. Hell, if it exists, is for evil people like Hitler. Live a good life; that's the key." But as the Bible warns, "There is a way that seems right to a man, but its end is the way of death" (Proverb 14:12).

LEARN FROM JEREMIAH

Jeremiah is often called the weeping prophet. The passionate warnings he gave to his sinful generation came with tears. He was a direct mouthpiece for God:

> "Your own wickedness will correct you,
> and your backslidings will rebuke you.
> Know therefore and see that it is an evil and
> bitter thing
> that you have forsaken the LORD your God,
> and the fear of Me is not in you,"
> says the Lord GOD of hosts. (Jeremiah 2:19)

God told Israel that forsaking him was sinful. It was an evil and bitter thing. He gave them life itself, so for his people to turn their backs on him was more than evil—it was a "bitter" evil that left them without the fear of God: "And the fear of Me is not in you." He also used the word *wickedness* to describe their actions. Few things nowadays are called "wicked." Not adultery, not fornication, not lying or stealing or blasphemy. Morality has been redefined. We may change the nature of sin, negate its consequences, or mock it, but its wages stay the same. It pays us in death and eventually in damnation.

God told Israel, "Your own wickedness will correct you." While that can be interpreted as a threat, it is also a loving warning. It is a warning sign saying that the road of sin leads to a washed-out bridge and a grisly two-hundred-foot drop. If someone takes heed of the notice and turns around, the warning does them a great favor.

LEARN FROM JESUS

When we came to the Savior, we put on the yoke of discipleship and began taking our direction from Jesus, who said, "Take My yoke upon you and learn from Me, for I am gentle and lowly in heart, and you will find rest for your souls" (Matthew 11:29). So, when it comes to reaching the lost, he is our teacher and our example. When Jesus warned the wicked about their wickedness, he showed them that their building was on fire. That's what love does. Let's now sit at his feet and learn from him.

Jesus begins his Sermon on the Mount by defining godly character and speaking directly to our mission—to be peacemakers between people and God (see Matthew 5:9). He warns that as preachers of the gospel of peace, we will be persecuted (vv. 10–12). We are also to be the light of the world (v. 14). Without the light of a clear gospel proclamation, the world will remain in darkness. People will continue to go about establishing their own righteousness while being ignorant of the righteousness that is of God. The teacher of all teachers then gives us instruction on how to fill the sinner's room with smoke, so to speak:

> Do not think that I came to destroy the Law or the Prophets. I did not come to destroy but to fulfill. For assuredly, I say to you, till heaven and earth pass away, one jot or one tittle will by no means pass from the law till all is fulfilled. Whoever therefore breaks one of the least of these commandments, and teaches men so, shall be called least in the kingdom of heaven; but whoever does and teaches them, he shall be called great in the kingdom of heaven. For I say to you, that unless your righteousness exceeds the righteousness of the scribes and Pharisees, you will by no means enter the kingdom of heaven. (vv. 17–20)

We are to do what Jesus did: expound the law and teach sinners the Ten Commandments. If we do that, we will be called great in the kingdom of heaven (v. 19). That's what Daniel did in Belshazzar's court. It's also what John the Baptist did. He was faithful in his preaching, and Jesus called him the greatest prophet born of women (Luke 7:28). John didn't hesitate to tell a king he was violating God's law through his adultery: "For Herod himself had sent and laid hold of John, and bound him in prison for the sake of Herodias, his brother Philip's wife; for he had married her. Because John had said to Herod, 'It is not lawful for you to have your brother's wife'" (Mark 6:17–18).

If you want God's smile, imitate Jesus and use the law as a schoolteacher to instruct sinners (see Galatians 3:24). David understood this was one of the purposes of the law. In the Psalms, he wrote, "Good and upright is the LORD; Therefore *He teaches sinners in the way*" (Psalm 25:8, emphasis added). And in another psalm, he prayed:

> Restore to me the joy of Your salvation,
> and uphold me by Your generous Spirit.
> *Then I will teach transgressors Your ways*,
> and sinners shall be converted to You.
> (51:12–13, emphasis added)

We are to instruct transgressors by putting the righteousness required by God far from their grasp, stripping them of false hope. This is what Jesus did with his hearers. He said that unless their righteousness exceeded the righteousness of the scribes and Pharisees, they would by no means enter the kingdom of heaven. How could anyone become more righteous than the scribes and Pharisees? Their outward appearance was pure; they were like clean and white sepulchers (Matthew 23:27). But theirs wasn't the righteousness that delivers from death.

Jesus then placed the righteousness needed to live even further from the grasp of his hearers by telling them God required truth in their inward parts (see Psalm 51:6). For example, he didn't just condemn murder; he condemned those who desire to murder:

> You have heard that it was said to those of old, "You shall not murder, and whoever murders will be in danger of the judgment." But I say to you that whoever is angry with his brother without a cause shall be in danger of the judgment. And whoever says to his brother, "Raca!" shall be in danger of the council. But whoever says, "You fool!" shall be in danger of hell fire. (Matthew 5:21–22)

Jesus was showing the complacent sinner the flames through the window. Out of love, he continued to dash false hope and false peace by letting people know that not only does God condemn adultery, but he also condemns the desire to commit adultery. Then he compounded the condemnation by saying what they should do with an eye or hand that betrayed them by leading them into lust:

> You have heard that it was said to those of old, "You shall not commit adultery." But I say to you that whoever looks at a woman to lust for her has already committed adultery with her in her heart. If your right eye causes you to sin, pluck it out and cast it from you; for it is more profitable for you that one of your members perish, than for your whole body to be cast into hell. And if your right hand causes you to sin, cut it off and cast it from you; for it is more profitable for you that one of your members perish, than for your whole body to be cast into hell. (vv. 27–30)

Listen to Jesus as he permanently pulls the hope of salvation from our grasp by making salvation by works completely unobtainable. In no uncertain terms, he tells all who can hear, "Be perfect" (v. 48)— be as morally perfect as God himself. The sinner's room is filled with smoke. His only way of escape is through the door of mercy.

JESUS IS THE DOOR OF MERCY

In the face of his sin, the sinner must get low, smite his breast, and cry, "God, be merciful to me, a sinner!" There is no other way to flee the flames: "How shall we escape if we neglect so great a salvation?" (Hebrews 2:3). Consider this warning call Charles Spurgeon issued to those who thought they had the right key of escape:

> If you can sin and not weep over it, you are an heir of Hell! If you can go into sin, and afterwards feel satisfied to have done so, you are on the road to destruction! If there are no pricks of conscience, no inward torments, no bleeding wounds—if you have no throbs and heaves of a bosom that cannot rest—if your soul never feels filled with wormwood and gall when you know you have done evil—you are no child of God.[40]

When I read quotes from Charles Spurgeon as he pleaded with the lost, I hear love in his tone. How I would love to have heard the tone of Jesus' voice as he warned people! God has placed something within the hearts of sinners that can detect the sound of concern. Amidst the flames, the tone of your voice can spark a mustard seed of belief in their hearts, and if they believe your warning, they will flee the flames. They are not beasts. God has made them in his image and placed his law within them so that they can know when truth is present.

The law exposes evil, and that should result in the fear of the Lord. And it is "by the fear of the LORD one departs from evil" (Proverbs 16:6). Therefore, we must lift up our voices, shout from the housetops, smash the windows, break down the doors, grab sinners by the sleeve—whatever it takes to pull them from the fire—to show them the wondrous mercy God has provided for us on the cross. We all deserve the punishment of death because we cannot live in obedience to a holy God. We need the fear of the Lord to realize Jesus is the only way to a real relationship with the Creator of the universe. While some people struggle with the idea that there is only one way to enter into this relationship, this thought should stir our hearts toward thankfulness: in his loving mercy, God has provided us the Way. Because of Jesus, we can come near to God, who listens, provides, and blesses. There is no greater news than this. And in a hurting, sinful world, none more urgent.

WITNESSING ENCOUNTER

The following conversation was recorded at a college in Southern California. John was a very likable, long-haired atheist who (like all atheists) lacked the fear of God. But see what happened.

> RAY: John, what's the scariest thing that's happened to your life?
>
> JOHN: Birth.
>
> RAY: That was scary?
>
> JOHN: The aftermath was for sure.
>
> RAY: You remember it?
>
> JOHN: No.
>
> RAY: You talking about life itself?
>
> JOHN: Yes, sir.
>
> RAY: Yes, life is scary. We do walk through the valley of the shadow of death. At any moment, friends and loved ones or even your dog can be ripped from you by death. Life is fearful. Have you ever had a nightmare that leaves you sweating, with your heart pounding in your chest, and you think about it for the next ten to twenty minutes?
>
> JOHN: Not necessarily, no, but I do remember occasions of waking up, trying to discern what was what.
>
> RAY: Now, you're an atheist?
>
> JOHN: Yes, sir.

RAY: We'll talk about that in a minute. Let me just give you a quick scenario. You wake up one morning, and there's a lump under your arm. And you think, *Man, this really hurts!* So you go straight to the doctor, and he looks at it, looks very concerned, and he says, "This looks serious." He comes back after tests and says, "This is lymph node cancer. It's metastasized. You are going to be dead in two weeks. I'm so sorry. Here's some drugs to ease the pain. They can have side effects, but they'll help you." You get home, and you're lying in bed not thinking of sex or being with friends or partying. You are nauseated horribly, and you're thinking to yourself, *What's going to happen after I die? Is there an afterlife?*

Have you ever asked that question? And this is not an unrealistic scenario. Six-hundred thousand Americans will die of cancer in the next year, and 8.2 million people worldwide, just of cancer. So, this is very realistic. Does that scenario kind of scare you, or are you just blasé about it?

JOHN: A little. Knowing that I'm going to die soon as opposed to knowing I could die any second, but you know, it is what it is.

RAY: That is a funny thought, you just said. It's scarier to know that in two weeks you're going to be dead than in the next few minutes. It's because we really don't believe we could die in the next five minutes. Death is what happens to *other* people. I'm going to give you another scenario, just to prep you for something. If I put you on a thousand-foot cliff, right on the edge, where your toes are over and you can feel the stones crumbling beneath your feet, would that be fearful for you?

JOHN: Definitely.

RAY: Would that be a good feeling or a bad feeling?

JOHN: It would be terrifying

RAY: A horrible, tormenting fear. But there is another aspect. The fear would be good because it's telling you to move back from the cliff—that you're in danger. And so your fear is not your enemy; it's your friend in that respect. You are an atheist, so I'm going to try and give you a fear that's your friend because you've got an image of God that's erroneous. Tell me, what do you think God is like?

JOHN: If he is all-powerful and all-good, why do we have things such as massive disasters like volcanoes or earthquakes?

RAY: That is a good question. The Bible gives a clear answer. We live in a fallen creation. God is angry at the world because of sin, and all these things show us we live in a fallen creation—earthquakes, floods, famines, tornadoes, hurricanes, disease, and death are all stark realities that what the Bible says is true—that we live in a fallen creation. Why are you an atheist?

JOHN: I cannot grasp my head around that fact that if there is an all-loving God…children are baptized because they are born with sin. Correct?

RAY: The Bible says to repent and be baptized because *all* are sinful. Therein (in what you said) is the problem—where you said that you can't figure out how an all-loving God can allow the suffering of a child. God's not all-loving. The Bible doesn't say that. It's like saying to a judge when you stand in front of him, "I raped the woman and cut her throat, but you're all-loving. How come you're angry at me?" He would say, "I'm not all-loving." In fact, a judge has to set aside his love when he judges a trial. He can't say, "This is my brother-in-law. I love him."

No, he can't pervert justice. [BRIEF PAUSE] So, you are an atheist. Do you really believe the scientific impossibility that nothing created everything? Surely, you can't believe that.

JOHN: Scientists are working on what happened before the big bang. But before that, I draw a blank.

RAY: So, do you think there was a creative force of some sort? It just wasn't God?

JOHN: I sure hope so.

RAY: Therefore, you're not an atheist; you're agnostic. You know there was something in the beginning—you just don't know what it was. Does that make sense?

JOHN: Yes, that makes sense.

RAY: Let's see if we can move you from atheism, to agnosticism, to theism. When you look at a building, how do you know there was a builder?

JOHN: Someone had to put it there.

RAY: Yes, buildings don't build themselves. Creation proves there is a Creator. You can see the genius of God's creative hand in flowers, birds, trees, the sun, the moon, the stars, the marvels of the human eye, and male and female in all the different species. [BRIEF PAUSE] So, do you think God is angry at you or happy with you?

JOHN: I would say we are insignificant. So if there is a God, he would be unbothered or indifferent because there's just so much going on, how could he keep track of all of it?

RAY: Well, he made every single atom that makes up your eye—which has 137 million light cells. He sees the atom from inside out because he made it. There is order from the atom to the universe. He made your heart, your liver, your kidneys, your lungs—all with independent functions. And so he's intimately familiar with you as a person. Every long hair on your head is numbered by God. Did you know that?

JOHN: I did not.

RAY: Yes, because he made every one. And it's living, and it grows, and it gets fed by the food you eat. That is where it gets its substance from. We are fearfully and wonderfully made. So, do you think you are a good person?

JOHN: I try to be.

RAY: How many lies have you told in your life?

JOHN: How many lies have I told today? [Expletive]!

RAY: You just blasphemed God's name.

JOHN: Heck, yes. I didn't want to say "hell."

RAY: So, you've told lies. What do you call someone who tells lies?

JOHN: A human being.

RAY: What would you call me if I told lies?

JOHN: A liar.

RAY: It's hard to say about yourself, isn't it? We find it hard to judge ourselves.

[I then took John through the Ten Commandments. When I asked him if he would be guilty on judgment day, he said he would be guilty and would end up in hell. When I asked him if that concerned him, he said it did. That surprised me. He said it was because he was brought up as a Catholic but could not reconcile what he saw in the world with what he had been taught. I told him not to throw out the baby with the bathwater, that there is something of substance among all the confusion in the contemporary church. When I asked John what God did for guilty sinners, he said, "He sacrificed his only Son." I then explained the cross and the need for repentance and faith.]

RAY: I've so appreciated you giving me an ear and listening to what I'm saying. You don't realize this, but I love you, and I care about you, and the thought of you ending up in hell horrifies me. I have tried the best I could to hang you over the cliffs of eternity and show you that it's a fearful thing to fall into God's hands, hoping that you will see fear as your friend and not your enemy. I'm not trying to win an argument. I'm not trying to say I defeated an atheist. I'm trying to say, "Man, I love you, and I want to see you in heaven and not in hell." So, does this make sense?

JOHN: Yes, it does!

RAY: Are you going to think about what we talked about?

JOHN: Probably.

Chapter 9

PROMISES TO THOSE WHO FEAR GOD

Welcome to another day on planet earth—a day of plagues, earthquakes, tornadoes, hurricanes, famines, fires, floods, droughts, and untold human suffering—where evil routinely triumphs over good. All of these phenomena are evidence that we live in a fallen creation, as revealed to us in the first three chapters of the book of Genesis.

Welcome also to another day of seeing the Bible's amazing prophecies coming to pass—where people's hearts fail them for fear of what's coming next (see Luke 21:25–28). The reason people's hearts fail them is that they don't believe anyone is in control. If they could take control, they wouldn't be fearful. But those who fear God know that he is *always* in control. He's never taken by surprise or thrown into confusion. Oswald Chambers said, "The remarkable thing about God is that when you fear God, you fear nothing else, whereas if you do not fear God, you fear everything else."[41]

If we fear the Lord, we will have faith in him—because we dare not insult him with the slightest unbelief. And we will then have joy and peace in believing. If we fear the Lord, we will divorce ourselves from evil (see Proverbs 16:6).

Psalm 112 describes the godly character of someone who fears God and the promises the Lord makes to such a person: "Blessed is the man who fears the LORD, who delights greatly in His commandments" (v. 1). In other words, if we have the fear of the Lord, it will be evidenced by our joyful obedience to God's will. We will say, "I delight to do Your will, O my God, and Your law is within my heart" (Psalm 40:8). Here now, from Psalm 112, are the blessings promised to you if you fear the Lord and esteem his law:

- Your children will be blessed: "His descendants will be mighty on earth; the generation of the upright will be blessed" (v. 2).

- You will be blessed: "Wealth and riches will be in his house" (v. 2).

- You will have everlasting righteousness in Christ: "And his righteousness endures forever" (v. 3).

- God's Word will be a lamp to your feet and a light to your path: "Unto the upright there arises light in the darkness" (v. 4).

- The fruit of the Spirit will be evidenced in your life: "He is gracious, and full of compassion, and righteous" (v. 4).

- You will be free from the love of money: "A good man deals graciously and lends" (v. 5).

- You will be law-abiding: "He will guide his affairs with discretion" (v. 5).

- Your life will be built on the teachings of Jesus, the foundation that stands firm in life's storms: "Surely he will never be shaken" (v. 6).

- You will never be forgotten by God: "The righteous will be in everlasting remembrance" (v. 6).

- You will fear no evil, nor will you fear the future because Jesus will never leave you nor forsake you: "He will not be afraid of evil tidings; his heart is steadfast, trusting in the LORD. His heart is established; he will not be afraid, until he sees his desire upon his enemies" (vv. 7–8).

- You will be rich in good works: "He has dispersed abroad, he has given to the poor" (v. 9).

- The righteousness you have in Christ will deliver you from death and give you entrance into the kingdom of God: "His righteousness endures forever; his horn will be exalted with honor. The wicked will see it and be grieved; he will gnash his teeth and melt away; the desire of the wicked shall perish" (vv. 9–10).

The same God who will fulfill his promise to judge the world will fulfill his promise to bless those who fear the Lord. The choice is ours. We can disobey and let sin rule in our lives, or we can trust God in obedience and come to him in prayer.

THE BLESSING OF PRAYER

Have you ever thought about the privilege and power of prayer? God Almighty, the all-knowing, all-powerful Creator of the universe, invites his children to enter into his presence to offer their thanksgiving and share their needs. And yet, our prayer may be a simple thought. Or it may be just one desperate word in a dire emergency: "Help!" That's the great comfort we have when it comes to prayer. It is never our words that make it effective.

Jesus' prayers were heard because he feared God. The fear he had was transformed into action through his personal obedience to the will of the Father. Scripture speaks of his obedience—and the necessity of our own:

> [Christ], in the days of His flesh, when He had offered up prayers and supplications, with vehement cries and tears to Him who was able to save Him from death, and was heard because of His godly fear, though He was a Son, yet He learned obedience by the things which He suffered. And having been perfected, *He became the author of eternal salvation to all who obey Him.* (Hebrews 5:7–9, emphasis added)

We have God's promise that because of our holy fear and corresponding obedience, God will hear our prayers. Even so, our fear does not guarantee the outcome we desire. God always has his purposes in mind when he responds to the prayers of those who love him—and his ways are not our ways:

> "For My thoughts are not your thoughts,
> nor are your ways My ways," says the LORD.
> "For as the heavens are higher than the earth,
> so are My ways higher than your ways,
> and My thoughts than your thoughts." (Isaiah 55:8–9)

Sometimes we will see an immediate response to our requests, and other times we may not see any response. Both outcomes are answers to prayer. We know the prayers of Jesus were always heard (John 11:42), but he didn't always get the result he desired. In the garden of Gethsemane, he knelt down and earnestly prayed, saying, "Father, if it is Your will, take this cup away from Me; nevertheless not My will, but Yours, be done" (Luke 22:42).

Jesus didn't want to suffer. He wanted the imminent suffering of the cross to be removed from him. He said, "Take this cup away from Me." But his Father didn't grant him that request, so Jesus yielded his will to his Father's. If we walk in the fear of the Lord, that's the attitude we will bring with us as we make our requests known to God: "Be anxious for nothing, but in everything by prayer and supplication, with thanksgiving, let your requests be made known to God" (Philippians 4:6).

Praying with childlike trust relieves us of anxiety. If we don't get our desired result, we can, like Jesus, yield our will to God's will. And because we have seen his love expressed at the cross, we will take consolation that he is in control, even in the darkest valleys of life:

Who shall separate us from the love of Christ? Shall tribulation, or distress, or persecution, or famine, or nakedness, or peril, or sword? As it is written:

> "For Your sake we are killed all day long; we are accounted as sheep for the slaughter."

Yet in all these things we are more than conquerors through Him who loved us. For I am persuaded that neither death nor life, nor angels nor principalities nor powers, nor things present nor things to come, nor height nor depth, nor any other created thing, shall be able to separate us from the love of God which is in Christ Jesus our Lord. (Romans 8:35–39)

Those who don't fear the Lord become disillusioned by heaven's silence because their understanding is darkened. But those who do fear the Lord and have received his mercy are no longer in the kingdom of darkness: "He has delivered us from the power of darkness and conveyed us into the kingdom of the Son of His love, in whom we have redemption through His blood, the forgiveness of sins" (Colossians 1:13–14).

We understand that although Jesus didn't get his desire, he *did* get his prayer answered. And even though we may not get what we request, we know we always have our prayers answered. God may remove the particular cross we are carrying, or he may leave it for us to haul a while longer. Three times the apostle Paul prayed about a certain thorny problem, and God denied his request three times:

> Lest I should be exalted above measure by the abundance of the revelations, a thorn in the flesh was given to me, a messenger of Satan to buffet me, lest I be exalted above measure. Concerning this thing I pleaded with the Lord three times that it might depart from me. And He said to me, "My grace is sufficient for you, for My strength is made perfect in weakness." (2 Corinthians 12:7–9)

Paul didn't get what he wanted, but he did get his prayer answered, and in essence responded, "Not my will, but yours, be done." It is with this mindset that we should approach the promises God has given us concerning the great treasure of the fear of the Lord: "Wisdom and knowledge will be the stability of your times, and the strength of salvation; the fear of the LORD is His treasure" (Isaiah 33:6).

THE BLESSING OF THE FEAR THE LORD

Let's now lift the lid off this treasure chest and pick up and examine four sparkling promises that come with fearing God:

1. The Promise of Deliverance

> The angel of the LORD encamps all around those who fear Him,
> and delivers them. (Psalm 34:7)

Again, we must be careful not to limit the deliverance that God promises to those who fear him. It *may* mean deliverance from some of the many temporal problems that surround us in this life, but it *certainly* means deliverance from the full consequences of death in the next. James wasn't delivered from Herod's sword (see Acts 12:2); neither was Stephen delivered from the stones that ushered him into eternity (see Acts 7:58). Yet God's love never left them, and they received their ultimate deliverance.

2. The Promise of Honor

> By humility and the fear of the LORD
> are riches and honor and life. (Proverbs 22:4)

> In whose eyes a vile person is despised,
> but he honors those who fear the LORD;
> he who swears to his own hurt and does not
> change. (Psalm 15:4)

God *will* honor you if you fear him and serve Jesus (see John 12:26). He may give you a long life, and perhaps he will entrust you with wealth. However, riches are not a blessing if they cause us to turn away from him. The words of Agur in the book of Proverbs are true wisdom in this regard: "Give me neither poverty nor riches—feed me with the food allotted to me; lest I be full and deny You, and say, 'Who is the Lord?'" (Proverbs 30:8–9).

Be careful of prosperity preachers who tell you that riches are your right—that God has promised you material blessings and that he, therefore, *owes* you wealth. Such an attitude disguises itself as faith, but it lacks both humility and the fear of God. When writing to Timothy, Paul warned him about the "useless wranglings of men of corrupt minds and destitute of the truth, who suppose that godliness is a means of gain. From such withdraw yourself" (1 Timothy 6:5).

The riches we should seek are those found in the blessing promised to those who fear the Lord. Remember, "For where your treasure is, there your heart will be also" (Matthew 6:21). The promise in this verse that Judas failed to see is that if your heart is in Jesus, your treasure is with him also. In him is your honor. Let this motivate your life.

3. The Promise of Contentment

Oh, fear the LORD, you His saints!
There is no want to those who fear Him.
(Psalm 34:9)

How good it is to be free from the distractions of greed and ambition! As Shakespeare put it, "By that sin fell the angels; how can man, then, the image of his Maker, hope to win by it?"[42] What a blessing—the fear of the Lord tames that deadly monster!

Look at this wonderful three-fold promise:

The fear of the LORD leads to life,
and he who has it will abide in satisfaction;
he will not be visited with evil. (Proverbs 19:23)

Contentment is a form of happiness this world seeks but misses. It is a wealth without riches. While ambition seeks joy from without, contentment finds it from within. It comes when righteousness in Christ is our priority. Without godly righteousness, we will perish on the day of wrath (see Proverbs 11:4).

Now godliness with contentment is great gain. For we brought nothing into this world, and it is certain we can carry nothing out. And having food and clothing, with these we shall be content. But those who desire to be rich fall into temptation and a snare, and into many foolish and harmful lusts which drown men in destruction and perdition. For the love of money is a root of all kinds of evil, for which some have strayed from the faith in their greediness, and pierced themselves through with many sorrows. (1 Timothy 6:6–10)

So many in this world are searching for satisfaction in earthly things that will never satisfy, yet those who fear the Lord possess a satisfaction that will never run dry because God has promised, "I will never leave you nor forsake you" (Hebrews 13:5). No matter what happens to us in this life, we can hold fast to this truth.

4. The Promise of Mercy

For as the heavens are high above the earth,
so great is His mercy toward those who fear Him;
as far as the east is from the west,
so far has He removed our transgressions from us.
As a father pities his children,
so the Lord pities those who fear Him…
But the mercy of the Lord is from everlasting
to everlasting
on those who fear Him,
and His righteousness to children's children.
(Psalm 103:11–13, 17)

Those who compromise the proclamation of the gospel by omitting the requirements of God's law, any mention of the day of judgment, or the reality of hell rob their hearers of the fear of the Lord. Remove God's wrath, and you hide his mercy. The law of God gives us an understanding of his fearful holiness and our own moral depravity, which then drives us to mercy and establishes us in the fear of the Lord. As long as I see his holiness, I will cling to the cross. If I lose sight of God's holiness through some form of subtle idolatry, I will fail to see my need of the blood shed for me on the cross.

> Do not be wise in your own eyes;
> fear the LORD and depart from evil.
> It will be health to your flesh,
> and strength to your bones. (Proverbs 3:7–8)

In the end, the fear of God is a blessing. It is a holy terror that drives us to our knees and replaces the selfishness native to our sinful hearts with a thirst for mercy and grace. It is a gift from God born out of love. Once again, the wisdom of Charles Spurgeon is helpful.

> When you really know God, you shall be thrice happy if you do run toward Him, falling down before Him, worshipping Him with bowed head

yet glad heart, all the while fearing toward Him, and not away from Him…

Again I say that we, who believe in Jesus, are not afraid of God even as our King, for He has made us also to be kings and priests, and we are to reign with Him, through Jesus Christ, forever and ever. Yet we tremble before Him lest we should be rebellious against Him in the slightest degree. With a childlike fear, we are afraid lest one revolting thought or one treacherous wish should ever come into our mind or heart to stain our absolute loyalty to Him. Horror takes hold upon us when we hear others deny that "the LORD reigneth," but even the thought that we should ever do this grieves us exceedingly, and we are filled with that holy fear, which moves us to obey every command of our gracious King so far as we know it to be His command.[43]

The fear of the Lord is our friend. Apart from Christ, we are lost in our sins—so lost we don't even know we need rescue. It is the fear of God, which comes to us when we rightly understand God and his nature, that sets us free to receive his mercy. Once in Christ, it is the fear of God that keeps us walking in the Spirit and abiding in Jesus—and our lives bear fruit to the glory of the Father (see John 15:1–8; Galatians 5:22–23).

When people fear God, they keep their hearts free from sin, and we do that by abiding in Christ. *He* is my righteousness. *He* is my confidence. *He* is my Lord and Savior, and when people—no matter who they are or what they've done—come to the Father fearing him and trusting in Jesus, they are heard by God. We have his immutable promise on that.

And there's nothing more certain.

WITNESSING ENCOUNTER

I offered a warm good morning to a gentleman who was working on a new stair railing at our ministry's headquarters. I noticed he was equally warm in his response, so when I saw him again a few minutes later, I asked his name, and we began a conversation.

RAY: John, do you think there's an afterlife?

JOHN: Yes, I think there is.

RAY: Why do you believe that?

JOHN: My upbringing.

RAY: How is your walk with the Lord at the moment?

JOHN: It could be better.

[When I asked him if he was reading his Bible, he said he hadn't for a long time. And then he added that he was a very busy person, working nearly twenty-four hours a day, seven days a week.]

RAY: Seven days a week? Why would you do that?

[He said that when he turned sixty, he wanted to have enough money to enjoy his retirement. He said that his wife was the same way.]

RAY: What happens if you die before you reach sixty? Who gets your money?

JOHN: I guess my wife will get it.

RAY: Jesus told a story about a man like you. He said that a man was so rich he decided to build bigger barns to keep all his goods in, and God said to him, "Fool! This night your soul will be required of you." Such are those who are not rich toward God [Luke 12:16–21]. John, this is your eternity. He gave you your wife, your eyesight, your freedom, your life, and you owe him to be first in your life. Jesus said that if you look at a woman and lust for her, you commit adultery with her in your heart [Matthew 5:28]. If you hate someone, you commit murder in your heart [v. 22]. That's how high God's standard is. No liar or thief will enter into God's kingdom. In fact, the Bible says sin is so serious in God's eyes that all liars it will be up at the lake of fire [Revelation 21:8]. That's why you need the cross. That's why you need Jesus as your Savior. There's nothing as important. Thank you for listening to me.

[He said it was no problem at all. I then gave him a couple of five-dollar gift cards, a signed book, and a little booklet called *How to Be Free from the Fear of Death*.[44]]

I have found that one key to sharing the gospel is to imagine that the people you're talking with are going to die that night. The odds are they won't, but the possibility is there, and if we love our neighbors as much as we love ourselves, we will be as concerned for their eternal salvation as much as we are for our own.

What student of Bible prophecy would deny that we are living in the closing hours of time? We are seeing Bible prophecy fulfilled before our eyes. However, here is one biblical sign of the end of the age that is often missed by those of us who are watching the signs of the times. Jesus said, "This gospel of the kingdom will be preached in all the world as a witness to all the nations, and then the end will come" (Matthew 24:14).

May God give us an end-time harvest—when the knowledge of the glory of the Lord covers the earth as the waters cover the sea (see Habakkuk 2:14). May it be our earnest prayer that in this hour of gross darkness, we would see the light of the glorious gospel shine like the sun breaking through dark storm clouds. Jesus also said, "The harvest truly is great, but the laborers are few; therefore pray the Lord of the harvest to send out laborers into His harvest" (Luke 10:2).

That's why we must make sure God hears our prayers. I hope that you're praying for laborers and that you are one of them. And I hope this book has helped to encourage you to that end.

ENDNOTES

1   A. W. Tozer, *The Knowledge of the Holy*, in *Three Spiritual Classics in One Volume* (Chicago: Moody Publishers, 2018), 125–26.

2   Stephen R. Miller, *Daniel*, vol. 18, The New American Commentary (Nashville, TN: Broadman & Holman Publishers, 1994), 140.

3   Steve Knaus, "The Final Party," Sapphire Sky (blog), October 7, 2016, https://sapphiresky.org/2016/10/07/the-final-party/.

4   Wikipedia, s.v. "Jeffrey Dahmer," last modified October 18, 2021, https://en.wikipedia.org/wiki/Jeffrey_Dahmer.

5   *Oxfordify Dictionary*, s.v. "evil (adj.)," accessed September 28, 2021, https://www.oxfordify.com/meaning/evil.

6   "What Is the Definition of Evil?" Got Questions, April 26, 2021, https://www.gotquestions.org/definition-of-evil.html.

7   Sarah Imgrund, "Religion Professors Argue Evangelical Christians Are White Racists Who 'May End Up Killing Us All,'" *The College Fix*, May 27, 2021, https://www.thecollegefix.com/religion-professors-argue-evangelical-christians-are-white-racists-who-may-end-up-killing-us-all/.

8   Will Maule, "Australian Rugby Team Kicks Out Star Player over 'Repent! Only Jesus Saves' Instagram Post," Faithwire, April 15, 2019, https://www.faithwire.com/2019/04/15/australian-rugby-team-kicks-out-star-player-over-repent-only-jesus-saves-instagram-post/.

9   D. L. Moody, "Where Art Thou?" Sermon Index, accessed September 28, 2021, https://www.sermonindex.net/modules/articles/index.php?view=article&aid=497.

10   Copies of *Counting the Days* are available at LivingWaters.com.

11   A. W. Pink, "Our Attitude towards God's Sovereignty," *Wicked Gate Magazine*, November 2020, https://www.wicketgate.co.uk/issue146/e146_4.html.

12   Albert Barnes, "Psalm 4:4," *Barnes' Notes on the Bible*, Bible Hub, accessed September 28, 2021, https://biblehub.com/commentaries/psalms/4-4.htm.

13   Pink, "Our Attitude."

14   Charles Haddon Spurgeon, "Noah's Faith, Fear, Obedience, and Salvation," transcript of sermon delivered at Metropolitan Tabernacle, London, UK, June 1, 1890, https://ftc.co/resource-library/blog-entries/when-faith-produces-fear/.

15   John Bunyan, *A Treatise on the Fear of God* (London, 1679), 5, PDF available at Mongerism, accessed September 28, 2021, https://www.monergism.com/thethreshold/sdg/bunyan/A_Treatise_on_the_Fear_of_God_-_John_Bunyan.pdf.

16   "Who Were the Chaldeans in the Bible?" Got Questions, April 26, 2021, https://www.gotquestions.org/Chaldeans.html.

17   Donovan Alexander, "15 Unusual Weather Phenomena That Are Hard to Come Across," Interesting Engineering, August 17, 2020, https://interestingengineering.com/15-unusual-weather-phenomena-that-are-hard-to-come-across.

18   "Benjamin Franklin's Last Great Quote and the Constitution," Constitution Daily, November 13, 2020, https://constitutioncenter.org/blog/benjamin-franklins-last-great-quote-and-the-constitution.

19   Daniel DeFoe, *The Political History of the Devil, As Well Ancient as Modern: In Two Parts* (London: Black Boy in Paternoster Row, 1726), 269, https://www.gutenberg.org/files/31053/31053-h/31053-h.htm.

20   Christopher Bullock, *The Cobler of Preston, a Farce* (London: S. Bladon, 1767), 21, PDF, https://ia802807.us.archive.org/0/items/coblerofprestonf00bull/coblerofprestonf00bull.pdf.

21   A. W. Tozer, *The Knowledge of the Holy*, in *Three Spiritual Classics in One Volume* (Chicago: Moody Publishers, 2018), 152.

22   Gilbert King, "The Candor and Lies of Nazi Officer Albert Speer," *Smithsonian Magazine*, January 8, 2013, https://www.smithsonianmag.com/history/the-candor-and-lies-of-nazi-officer-albert-speer-324737/.

23   "Josef Mengele, Known as the 'Angel of Death,' Dies," History, updated February 4, 2021, https://www.history.com/this-day-in-history/the-angel-of-death-dies.

24   Atika Shubert and Nadine Schmidt, "Most Nazis Escaped Justice. Now Germany Is Racing to Convict Those Who Got Away," CNN, updated December 15, 2018, https://www.cnn.com/2018/12/14/europe/germany-nazi-war-trials-grm-intl/index.html.

25   Charles Haddon Spurgeon, "The Peacemaker," The Spurgeon Center, transcript of sermon delivered at Metropolitan Tabernacle, London, UK, December 8, 1861, accessed January 31, 2022, https://www.spurgeon.org/resource-library/sermons/the-peacemaker/#flipbook/.

26   Copies of *The Bible's Four Gospels* are available at LivingWaters.com.

27   A. W. Tozer, excerpt from the essay "The Terror of the Lord," Acts 17:11 Bible Studies, accessed September 28, 2021, http://www.acts17-11.com/snip_tozer_terror.html.

28   John Bunyan, *A Treatise on the Fear of God* (London, 1679), 8, PDF available at Mongerism, accessed September 28, 2021, https://www.monergism.com/thethreshold/sdg/bunyan/A_Treatise_on_the_Fear_of_God_-_John_Bunyan.pdf.

29   Ron Carucci, "Why Ethical People Make Unethical Choices," *Harvard Business Review*, Business Ethics, December 16, 2016, https://hbr.org/2016/12/why-ethical-people-make-unethical-choices.

30   University of Maryland Medical Center, "Headphones Linked to Pedestrian Deaths, Injuries," ScienceDaily, accessed January 26, 2022, www.sciencedaily.com/releases/2012/01/120116200559.htm.

31   Linda Thrasybule, "Injuries, Deaths Rise for Pedestrians Wearing Headphones," May 30, 2013, https://www.livescience.com/36092-injuries-deaths-pedestrians-wearing-headphones.html.

32   *Oxfordify Dictionary*, s.v. "alarm (n.)," accessed September 28, 2021, https://www.oxfordify.com/meaning/alarm.

33   Martyn Lloyd-Jones, "A Fear of the Lord," MLJTrust, YouTube video, 53:22, May 25, 2017, https://youtu.be/3X-XaTJ7XHc.

34   Yaroslav Trofimov and Felicia Schwartz, "As Hamas Rockets Rain on Israel, Iron Dome Proves It Can Withstand the Barrages," *The Wall Street Journal*, updated May 16, 2021, https://www.wsj.com/articles/as-hamas-rockets-rain-on-israel-iron-dome-proves-it-can-withstand-the-barrages-11621180126.

35   Copies of *Save Yourself Some Pain* are available at LivingWaters.com.

36   This tradition of respecting the divine name by translating it with a form of "Lord" can still be seen in most English Bibles today. Whenever you see *Lord* in small capital letters in the Old Testament, the Hebrew word being translated is *YHWH*, pronounced "YAHWEH."

37   *A King James Dictionary,* s.v. "Rabbi (n.)," accessed September 28, 2021, https://www.biblestudytools.com/dictionary/rabbi/. Technically, *Rabbi* can also mean "my master" and was often used as a title of respect, but the term carries much less weight than does *Lord*.

38   George Whitefield, "A Penitent Heart, the Best New Year's Gift," in *Selected Sermons of George Whitefield,* accessed December 13, 2021, https://www.ccel.org/ccel/whitefield/sermons.xxxiv.html.

39   Charles Haddon Spurgeon, "A Fear to Be Desired," transcript of sermon delivered at Metropolitan Tabernacle, London, UK, November 7, 1878, PDF, https://www.spurgeongems.org/sermon/chs2801.pdf.

40   Charles Haddon Spurgeon, *Spurgeon's Sermons, Vol. 13: 1867*, ed. Anthony Uyl (Woodstock, ON: Devoted Publishing, 2017), 401.

41   Oswald Chambers, *The Highest Good with The Pilgrim's Song Book and Thy Great Redemption* (Grand Rapids, MI: Discovery House, 1965), 537.

42   William Shakespeare, *Henry VIII*, 3.2.520–522, Folger Shakespeare Library, accessed September 28, 2021, https://shakespeare.folger.edu/shakespeares-works/henry-viii/act-3-scene-2/.

43   Charles Haddon Spurgeon, "A Fear to Be Desired," transcript of sermon delivered at Metropolitan Tabernacle, London, UK, November 7, 1878, PDF, https://www.spurgeongems.org/sermon/chs2801.pdf.

44   Copies of *How to Be Free from the Fear of Death* are available at LivingWaters.com.

ABOUT THE AUTHOR

Ray Comfort is the best-selling author of more than one hundred books. He is the cohost of an award-winning television program that airs in 190 countries and the producer of award-winning movies that have been viewed by millions (see www.FullyFreeFilms.com). He lives in Southern California with his wife, Sue, and has three grown children. For more information, visit LivingWaters.com.